**75 More Movie Moments
to Get Teenagers Talking**

Videos That Teach 3

DOUG FIELDS & EDDIE JAMES

Youth Specialties

ZONDERVAN™

GRAND RAPIDS, MICHIGAN 49530 USA

WWW.ZONDERVAN.COM

Youth Specialties

Videos That Teach 3
Copyright © 2004 by Youth Specialties

Youth Specialties Books, 300 South Pierce Street, El Cajon, CA 92020, are published
by Zondervan, 5300 Patterson Avenue SE, Grand Rapids, MI 49530

Library of Congress Cataloging-in-Publication Data

Fields, Doug, 1962-
  Videos that teach 3 : 75 more movie moments to get teenagers talking /
by Doug Fields and Eddie James.
    p. cm.
  ISBN 0-310-25107-9 (pbk.)
  1. Motion pictures in Christian education. 2. Christian education of
teenagers. I. Title: Videos that teach three. II. James, Eddie, 1970-
III. Title.
  BV1535.4.F55 2004
  268'.67--dc22

                                                                    2003017369

Unless otherwise indicated, all Scripture quotations are taken from the Holy Bible:
New International Version (North American Edition). Copyright © 1973, 1978, 1984
by International Bible Society. Used by permission of Zondervan.

Web site addresses listed in this book were current at the time of publication. Please
contact Youth Specialties via e-mail (YS@YouthSpecialties.com) to report URLs that
are no longer operational and replacement URLs if available.

Editing by Sally Harris
Printed in the United States of America

04 05 06 07 08 09 / DC / 10 9 8 7 6 5 4 3 2 1

Acknowledgments

Thanks to Ted Lowe, Tommy Woodard, Cathy Fields, Stephanie James, Mike Gwartney, Eddie Walker, Brian Cropp, and Dennis Beckner.

Special thanks to Erin MacDonald, Charissa Fishbeck, Andy Brazelton, Linda Kaye, and Sally Harris.

—Doug and Eddie

Contents

The movies (in alphabetical order)

Quick Clip Locator

BY TOPIC

Conviction   Hart's War; Legally Blonde
Courage   Hart's War; Joe Somebody; Moonlight Mile
Courtesy   Kate and Leopold
Covering for others   I Am Sam
Creativity   The Best Bits of Mr. Bean
Danger   Pearl Harbor
Dating   Singles
Death   Tuck Everlasting
Decisions   Changing Lanes
Defeat   Pearl Harbor
Denial   Sweet Home Alabama
Desire   The Rookie
Destiny   Life or Something Like It; The Princess Diaries; Serendipity
Determination   Men of Honor; The Sum of All Fears
Dignity   Joe Somebody; Maid in Manhattan
Direction   Bedazzled
Dissention   We Were Soldiers
Distraction   Bedazzled; For the Love of the Game
Divine appointments   The Four Feathers
Divine intervention   Signs
Divorce   Crossroads
Doing the right thing   Spiderman
Doubt   Count of Monte Cristo
Dreams   The Rookie; Tucker: The Man and His Dreams
Drugs   Minority Report
Duty   Hart's War
Embarrassment   Joe Somebody
Emotional numbness   Mr. Deeds
Empowerment   Almost Famous
Encouragement   The Lord of the Rings: The Fellowship of the Ring (1st clip);
   Men of Honor
Endurance   Men of Honor
Enemy   The Recruit
Escaping the past   Insomnia; Sweet Home Alabama
Estranged relationships   The Last Castle
Evangelism   The Big Kahuna; A Walk to Remember
Evil   The Mothman Prophecies; White Oleander
Excuses   Monsters, Inc.
External versus internal character   Austin Powers in Goldmember
Eye for an eye   K-PAX
Faith   Count of Monte Cristo; Legally Blonde
False appearances   Shrek
Family   About a Boy; Antwone Fisher; Crossroads; Ice Age
Fate   Serendipity
Father   The Last Castle
Father-daughter relationships   What Women Want
Fear   The Four Feathers; The Lord of the Rings: The Fellowship of the Ring
   (1st clip); Monsters, Inc.; Panic Room
Feelings   Adaptation
First impressions   My Big Fat Greek Wedding
Focus   For the Love of the Game
Foolishness   My Big Fat Greek Wedding
Forgiveness   Changing Lanes; The Divine Secrets of the Ya Ya Sisterhood
Free will   Jimmy Neutron: Boy Genius
Freedom   Jimmy Neutron: Boy Genius
Friendship   Adaptation; Crossroads; Ice Age

Future   The Emperor's Club; The Rookie
Getting caught   Big Fat Liar
Gifts   The Rookie
Girls and boys   What Women Want
Giving   With Honors
God   Bedazzled; The Four Feathers
God's power   Unbreakable
God's voice   Hometown Legend; Life or Something Like It
God's will   Bedazzled; Hometown Legend; Trains, Planes, and Automobiles
God's Word   The Mothman Prophecies
Godliness   John Q
Good versus evil   Bedazzled; The Recruit; Trains, Planes, and Automobiles
Government   K-PAX
Grace   Tucker: The Man and His Dreams
Gray areas   Insomnia; The Recruit
Growth   Unbreakable
Guilt   Disney's The Kid; Insomnia
Hatred   Remember the Titans
Heartache   Crossroads; Dragonfly
Heaven   Dragonfly
Hell   Dragonfly
Heritage   Antwone Fisher
Hidden power   Unbreakable
High school   Adaptation
Home   The Lord of the Rings: The Fellowship of the Ring (1st clip)
Homelessness   With Honors
Homosexuality   Far from Heaven
Honesty   Remember the Titans
Honor   Hart's War
Hope   Men of Honor
Human spirit   Men of Honor
Humanity   K-PAX
Image   Shallow Hal
Impatience   The Four Feathers
Impossibilities   Pearl Harbor
Information   The Sum of All Fears
Innate behavior versus lifestyle choices   Far from Heaven
Inner beauty   Shallow Hal
Insecurity   Joe Somebody
Integrity   Drumline
Isolation   About a Boy
Judgment   Changing Lanes; Maid in Manhattan
Justice   Count of Monte Cristo
Knowledge   The Mothman Prophecies
Laws   K-PAX
Leadership   Remember the Titans
Legacy   Catch Me If You Can; The Emperor's Club; Eye for an Eye; Remember the Titans
Letting go   Disney's The Kid
Lies   Big Fat Liar; I Am Sam; Sweet Home Alabama
Life   Tuck Everlasting
Life purpose   Life or Something Like It
Lifestyle   A Walk to Remember
Listening   For the Love of the Game
Living an extraordinary life   Tuck Everlasting
Living in darkness   Big Trouble

Religious denominations   Meet the Parents
Religious wars   The Siege
Reputation   Count of Monte Cristo
Rescue   Count of Monte Cristo
Respect   Kate and Leopold; Remember the Titans
Responsibility   Clockstoppers; Drumline; The Princess Diaries; The Sum of All Fears
Revenge   Eye for an Eye
Right versus wrong   The Recruit
Risk   The Lord of the Rings: The Fellowship of the Ring (1st clip)
Rituals   The Best Bits of Mr. Bean
Running away   The Four Feathers
Sacrifice   Hart's War; Ice Age; John Q; The Rookie; With Honors
Sadness   Minority Report
Safety   The Lord of the Rings: The Fellowship of the Ring (1st clip); Panic Room
Satan   Bedazzled; We Were Soldiers
Second chances   The Last Castle
Secrets   Far from Heaven
Self-esteem   Shallow Hal
Selfishness   About a Boy; The Lord of the Rings: The Fellowship of the Ring (2nd clip)
Self-respect   Shallow Hal
Self-worth   Antwone Fisher
Sense of self   Legally Blonde
Serendipity   Serendipity
Serving one another   About a Boy; Maid in Manhattan; With Honors
Sex   Singles; What Women Want
Shallowness   Shallow Hal
Shame   Tucker: The Man and His Dreams
Significance   Maid in Manhattan
Signs   Serendipity
Sin   Big Trouble
Sincerity   The Big Kahuna; Meet the Parents
Socialization   K-PAX
Solitude   For the Love of the Game
Soul mates   Serendipity
Spiritual gifts   Catch Me If You Can
Spiritual power   The Mothman Prophecies
Spiritual substance   Almost Famous
Spiritual warfare   We Were Soldiers
Spiritually equipped   The Mothman Prophecies
Standards   Changing Lanes
Stereotypes   A Walk to Remember
Strength   Unbreakable
Strongholds of sin   The Lord of the Rings: The Fellowship of the Ring (2nd clip)
Substance   Maid in Manhattan
Suicide   Dragonfly
Supreme being   Signs
Talent   Big Fat Liar; Catch Me if You Can; The Rookie
Teamwork   Drumline
Temptation   The Lord of the Rings: The Fellowship of the Ring (2nd clip)
Ten Commandments   K-PAX
Terrorism   The Siege
Testimony   Moonlight Mile
Tests   Unbreakable
Thoughtfulness   Kate and Leopold
Timing   The Big Kahuna

True love Shrek
Truth Big Fat Liar; Catch Me If You Can; I Am Sam; John Q; Maid in Manhattan; Moonlight Mile; Sweet Home Alabama
Ugliness Shrek
Unanswered questions Antwone Fisher
Unity Hometown Legend; Remember the Titans
Unknown Monsters, Inc.
Unlived life Tuck Everlasting
Unspoken words The Last Castle
Unworthiness Mr. Deeds
Usefulness Drumline
Values Changing Lanes; John Q; The Recruit; Shallow Hal
Vengeance Eye for an Eye
Victory Pearl Harbor
Vision Tucker: The Man and His Dreams
Vulnerability Monsters, Inc.; Moulin Rouge
War Pearl Harbor; The Siege; We Were Soldiers
Weaknesses Big Trouble; The Lord of the Rings: The Fellowship of the Ring (2nd clip)
Wealth Maid in Manhattan
Weariness Count of Monte Cristo
Willingness Drumline
Wisdom Eye for an Eye; Life or Something Like It
Words Meet the Parents; Mr. Deeds
Worrying about what others think Adaptation
Wounds The Legend of Bagger Vance

Quick Clip Locator

BY BIBLE REFERENCE

Genesis
2:18 . . . . . About a Boy; My Big Fat Greek Wedding
2:24 . . . . My Big Fat Greek Wedding
6:13-27 . . . . Legally Blonde
25:12-18 . . . . The Siege
50:20 . . . . Clockstoppers

Exodus
20:1-17 . . . . K-PAX
20:12 . . . . What Women Want

Leviticus
18:22 . . . . Far from Heaven
19:18 . . . . Eye for an Eye
20:13 . . . . Far from Heaven
24:19-20 . . . . Eye for an Eye

Deuteronomy
7:9 . . . . K-PAX
18:20 . . . . Life or Something Like It
20:4 . . . . Count of Monte Cristo; We Were Soldiers
30:19-20 . . . . Spiderman
31:6 The Lord of the Rings: The Fellowship of the Ring (1st clip); Panic Room
32:39 . . . . Dragonfly

Joshua
24:15 . . . . Spiderman

1 Samuel
16:7 Austin Powers in Goldmember; Shrek
17:47 . . . . Count of Monte Cristo

2 Samuel
11-12 . . . . Trains, Planes, and Automobiles
14:14 . . . . The Four Feathers

1 Chronicles
1:28 . . . . The Siege
29:11 . . . . Clockstoppers

2 Chronicles
15:7 . . . . The Lord of the Rings: The Fellowship of the Ring (1st clip)

Ezra
9:6 . . . . Insomnia

Esther
2:7-8:7 . . . . Legally Blonde

Job
1:7 . . . . The Mothman Prophecies
1:13-22 . . . . Count of Monte Cristo
16:19 . . . . Moonlight Mile
33:14-17 Tucker: The Man and His Dreams

Psalms
1:1 . . . . . . Trains, Planes, and Automobiles
5:7 . . . . The Best Bits of Mr. Bean
19:14 . . . . For the Love of the Game
23 . . . . We Were Soldiers
23:4 . . . . The Lord of the Rings: The Fellowship of the Ring (1st clip); The Mothman Prophecies; Panic Room
25:1 . . . . Bedazzled
25:12 . . . . Spiderman
27:4-6 . . . . Panic Room
27:10 . . . . Antwone Fisher; Crossroads
27:11 . . . . Trains, Planes, and Automobiles
30:4-5 . . . . . The Legend of Bagger Vance
32:5 . . . . Insomnia
33:1 . . . . The Best Bits of Mr. Bean
34:18 . . . . . Minority Report; Sweet Home Alabama
35:18 . . . . The Best Bits of Mr. Bean
38:4 . . . . Insomnia
42:5 . . . . Minority Report
43:18 . . . . . . The Legend of Bagger Vance
46:1 . . . . Unbreakable
46:10 . . . . For the Love of the Game
51:6 . . . . Big Fat Liar; I Am Sam; Moonlight Mile
55:22 . . . . . The Legend of Bagger Vance
61:3 . . . . Panic Room
68:5 . . . . Antwone Fisher
68:5-6 . . . . Crossroads
71:5 . . . . Adaptation
71:7 . . . . Unbreakable
91 . . . . Panic Room
91:14-15 . . . . Joe Somebody
94:12 . . . . Almost Famous
100:4 . . . . The Best Bits of Mr. Bean
101:7 . . . . Catch Me If You Can

A Note from Doug

Eddie and I are honored to have been given the opportunity to create another edition of *Videos That Teach*. This makes it a trilogy! We both love watching movies and communicating God's truth to students, which makes putting this resource together so much fun! Also, we've been blessed by the positive responses to the previous two volumes. Youth workers tell us story after story about how this resource helps improve their communication with students and assists in captivating their students' attention.

As a communicator, I am always looking for new ways to share the good news of Jesus Christ with students and believe that good teachers develop ways to use the changing world to communicate the unchanging nature of God. Since one of the most powerful and relevant mediums in our culture is film, I like to learn and teach this way. In some ways, movies have become the modern equivalent of storytelling (see "Esther, Everyman, and Ever After" in "How to use this book," page 21). The combination of moving images and narrative make a big impact on a message. The plot, the setting, and the dialogue all work together to create moments that either capture biblical truth or open the door to a person's heart. Many times, these clips communicate what I am trying to say much better than I can explain it.

These clips aren't only for explaining or emphasizing messages during a youth program; you can use them as discussion starters when you're just hanging out with students. One of the most powerful discussions I've had with teenagers happened after watching a movie—I just had some kids over, and we threw in a video. I didn't plan to use it as a teaching tool because getting these guys to talk was like pulling teeth, and watching a movie was the only thing I could think of doing with them. After the movie was over, I just asked a question, and the same guys who never paid any attention during small group (because they were usually wrestling) were all ears. We had an in-depth conversation about sin, redemption, and salvation. It was a great experience. I'm sure I could have gotten there without the clip, but it was a lot easier with it.

There is something wonderful in the moment when students realize their story is really God's story. When they begin to understand that the Bible is not a lifeless book but a personal narrative that includes them, their lives are changed. It's an honor for me to help you as you weave together these narrative moments into your teaching and your students' lives. My prayer is that they will continue to inspire and challenge the students in your church as well as provide opportunities for them to gain a deeper understanding of the Master Storyteller.

In the meantime…I'm still waiting for someone to write a book on strategies for returning videos on time!

19

Be careful!

Currently, I have a staff person who was fired from his previous church for showing a clip from an R-rated movie—ouch. I'm thrilled he's now working at Saddleback Church, but his means of arrival wasn't part of our strategy for recruiting interns! Be wise and preview each clip. Please be sure to read the FAQ: "Why are some clips in this book from R-rated movies?" (page 22)

A DVD idea

One additional suggestion that we haven't made in the other volumes is to use the subtitle option. If you are using DVD players to show the clips, turn on the subtitles in English. It's a powerful tool. Watching the clip while reading the dialogue is different from students' usual experiences, and it can help drive home a point that you are trying to use in your illustration or message, similar to showing the words of a song as it is played.

What's different about this book? (Important!)

In this book, getting to the actual clip is a little different from the first volume, but the same as in the second volume. **Instead of just putting in the video tape and having the VCR automatically set the counter to zero, you'll need to fast forward to the movie logo. Once you arrive at the movie logo (you'll usually see "This motion picture has been modified to fit your screen," right before the logo), hit "reset" on your counter, and fast forward to the start time listed in the book.**

How to Use This Book

So there I am, standing before a group of students, teaching a lesson about God's grace that I just knew would be unforgettable (after all, it took several hours to prepare—besides, it was one of those messages that would make my preaching professor proud...if he were still alive).

Halfway through my lesson, two guys in the back row start smacking each other. "Knock it off, jerk!" one of them says loudly.

Of course everyone turns around to see what's happening. I put on my Wounded Puppy Dog/Semi-Stern Pastor's Frown in a desperate attempt to communicate the hurt and disappointment I feel watching these two punks effectively kill the learning experience for everyone in the room. At the same time four girls near the front put their heads together and whisper something to each other. A guy slouching in the middle of the room yells out, "Hey, Doug, when will this sermon be over?" Then a girl from the whispering quartet runs out of the room crying.

So much for the unforgettable lesson about grace. My mind shifts to law, and I imagine sacrificing a few students on the altar of my frustration. I vow never to teach students again.

Yet within 48 hours the memories of yet another hellfest begin fading. I repress the pain of failure and begin looking (again) for fresh ways to teach next week from God's Word. Although inevitably a journey of pain and privilege, it's a journey that can be made a little easier by the book you're now holding.

Esther, Everyman, and Ever After

The ancient Hebrews told patriarchal stories. Jesus told parables. The medieval church staged morality plays. And Hollywood has become our culture's premiere storyteller. Stories, whether read, recited, or enacted, have always gripped people's imaginations and emotions.

Movies are today's parables. Theater attendance is at a record high, multiplexes are being built everywhere, and the movie industry is making more money than ever before. Even if these facts make you wince, you can still see how *Videos That Teach 3* uses movies—that is, visual storytelling—to launch meaningful discussions that go beyond the surface of the script to kids' spirits, discussions that get kids talking about themselves and life and God.

Why use movie clips in youth meetings, anyway?

Many of your students are visual learners—which means they'll be impacted more by seeing a message than by merely hearing it. And whether we like it or not, that's how most students seem to be learning these days, living in a culture saturated with visual media. An incessant, 24-hour stream of images on video, TV, movies, and the Internet surround us. Teenagers tend to be very comfortable with it all and respond well to it.

Which is why video makes perfect sense if you want to grab your students' attention.

And clips from videotaped movies are among those visual tools. For years Doug used object lessons, "spontaneous melodramas," and a variety of other creative teaching methods to reinforce his Bible teaching. He always wanted to use video clips but could never remember the right movie at the right time for the right message. His teaching changed when Eddie James joined him at Saddleback Church. Eddie—whose mind is a virtual storehouse of movie and video clips—would do a quick mental search on the topic Doug was to speak on and invariably come up with a clip to use. That gift of Eddie's quickly improved Doug's teaching and the students' interest.

FAQs

- **What about the copyright law?**
  Motion pictures are fully protected by copyright. Public exhibition, especially when an admission fee is charged, could violate copyright. The copyright doctrine of fair use, however, permits certain uses of brief excerpts from copyrighted materials for not-for-profit teaching purposes without permission. If you have specific questions about whether your plans to use film clips or other copyrighted materials in your lessons are permissible under these guidelines, you should consult your church's legal counsel. Or you or your church could apply for a blanket licensing agreement from The Motion Picture Licensing Corporation www.mplc.org for about $100 per year.

- **Why are some clips in this book from R-rated movies?***
  Because none of the clips in *Videos That Teach 3*, even those from R-rated movies, unless noted, contain language or content that is inappropriate or questionable to most youth groups.

  Because clips from R movies evoke very intense emotions and imagery.

  Because sometimes, carefully, you can teach good theology by pointing to bad theology.

  Because of course you'll preview whatever clip you want to use to make sure it's appropriate for your lesson and for your group.

  Because if, after you've previewed it, you're still unsure if it's

*Here are the 13 movies: Adaptation, Almost Famous, The Big Kahuna, Changing Lanes, Eye for an Eye, Hart's War, Insomnia, The Last Castle, Men of Honor, Panic Room, The Siege, Trains, Planes, and Automobiles, We Were Soldiers

suitable, you can always show it to your pastor, supervisor, or a parent for an opinion.

Because if you still don't feel comfortable using any of this book's 13 clips from R movies, there are still 62 clips that are G, PG, or PG-13.

Because movie ratings are assigned by the dozen or so members on the ratings board of the Motion Picture Association of America—www.mpaa.org—and the board's rating decisions are entirely subjective. The ratings board doesn't base its decisions on scriptural standards of conduct or art. Ratings simply advise viewers about the level of "adult" content in a movie so parents can exercise appropriate control over what their underage children see.

You get the point. The use of a clip in this book does not imply endorsement of the movie in general, of other scenes in that movie in particular, of the actors' lifestyles, of the use of animals, firearms, or Scripture quotations in the movie, of the manufacturer of the cars used in the chase scenes—in short, we're not endorsing anything. This book simply lists 75 short clips, most of which (but not all of which) are appropriate and instructive to most youth groups (but not all youth groups) in most situations (but not all situations).

So you make the call. You're an adult. You're a leader of your youth group's teenagers. You know at what point instruction becomes distraction—for you, for your students, for their parents, for your church or organization. Use the summaries—and preview the clip before the lesson!—to discern which movie clips are too sophisticated for your middle schoolers or too elementary for your senior highers. There's a lot to choose from here. Just think before you punch the play button.

- **Are you sure I need to preview a clip before showing it?**
If you don't preview a clip, you're asking for trouble—at the least it may cause you embarrassment, and at the most it may cost you your job. As you probably know, youth workers lose their jobs due to oversights like this. Protect yourself, preview the clip, and cue it up precisely.

Illustrating or building a lesson with *Videos That Teach 3*

Most youth workers use this book one of two ways:

- **You already have a lesson and want a clip to illustrate it.**
Great. Just flip to the "Quick Clip Locator—by topic" on page 7, find your topic, then turn to the corresponding clip. (If you're a browser, just leaf through the book with an eye on the upper-right corners of

the page spreads, where the topics of each clip are listed.) Or if your lesson is based on a Bible passage instead of a topic, check out the "Quick Clip Locator—by Bible reference" on page 13.

• *You simply want a change of pace in this week's youth meeting—and a movie-based lesson sounds good.* See the alphabetical list of movies in the table of contents for a movie you know and like, or just browse through the book until you find a clip that catches your interest.

What you'll find with each clip

Each of the 75 clips outlines in *Videos That Teach 3* contains the same parts, clip to clip. Use as many or as few of the parts as you need to take your lesson where you want it to go. You can use just the clip to illustrate your own lesson...you can build a full-blown Bible study around the clip with the Scripture references provided (and with preliminary study on your part!)...you can trigger small-group discussions with any of several questions for each clip (with considerably less preparation). You know your students, so adapt or scavenge accordingly to meet their needs.

Here are the parts each clip outline includes:

Trailer

This is the leading question or statement that gets kids' minds moving down the track of your topic (which are listed, by the way, in the upper-right corner of each clip's two-page spread). It gives you and your students an idea of what to watch and listen for as you view the clip.

For example, if you just jump into the clip, all you'll get are students reacting to the outcome—without paying attention to the source. On the other hand, if you set up your teaching time with a provocative question, students will still probably laugh at the clip—but underneath their laughter they'll get the point you're making. In fact, depending on how talkative a group you have, this opening question may trigger 15 or 20 minutes of discussion before you ever get to showing the clip.

The movie

If you're not familiar with a movie, this very brief summary helps you out. Even if you do know the movie, you can use (or read aloud) the summary to explain the storyline before you show a clip.

For a thorough, detailed description of the movie, get on the Web, type *movie reviews* into your favorite search engine, and choose one of the dozens of movie databases available. We found www.empireonline.co.uk/reviews particularly helpful. And www.screenit.com contains "entertainment reviews for parents" of videos (and movies, music, and DVDs) that not only summarize plot but list in detail why the movie received the rating it did, with categories like violence, alcohol/drugs, guns/weapons, blood/gore, disrespectful/bad attitude, sex/nudity, imitative behavior, topics to talk about, etc.

This clip

With this detailed description of the clip itself, we've also listed the start and stop times of the clip. Simply fast forward to the movie logo (you'll usually see "This motion picture has been modified to fit your screen" right before the movie logo), reset your counter to zero, and fast forward to the time where the clip begins. In case either the rental video or your VCR is different than ours, we've also included prompts from the movie—dialogue snippets or scene descriptions—to ensure that you start and stop it at the right time.

By the Book

The Bible is where you want your students to end up, sooner or later. If sooner, here's where you'll find Scriptures relevant to the clip's topic—to use for building a lesson from scratch or as biblical input or direction for small-group discussions.

Where to take it

Here are several discussion questions that generally try to bring together the clip's main point with its relevant Bible passages. Let the questions guide you, not coerce you. Tailor the questions to match the direction you want to take or guide the depth of discussion your kids are capable of. This is the time to help them explore the meanings behind the clip, how the Bible speaks to that particular situation, and how it all applies to them.

Keep on teaching!

About a Boy

The movie   comedy, PG-13

Will Lightman (Hugh Grant) takes pride in the fact that he is an island—no wife, no kids, no job, no problems. Will lives off the royalties of his late father's one-hit wonder Christmas song, and he divides his day into 30-minute increments because he doesn't want to commit to anything longer than that. Will dates a variety of women but is careful not to get too attached. Looking for a new way to pick up women, Will decides to pose as a single parent at a support group meeting and, unwittingly, steps into a world he is not prepared for. Will meets Marcus (Nicholas Hoault) who is tired of being an island—no dad, a suicidal mother, and no friends at school. Marcus decides that he wants Will to be a part of his family. Will is reluctant about about allowing Marcus into his island existence, but gradually the unlikely pair grows to care for and need each other.

This clip   (about 3 minutes)

▶ **Start** / 1:27:45 / "Excuse me? What is going on here?"

■ **Stop** / 1:33:00 / "Let's get off. Quick, get off."

Believing that he can help his mother out of her depression, Marcus decides to sing her favorite song, "Killing Him Softly," at the school talent show. When Will finds out his plan, he races to the school to stop Marcus and, he hopes, save the boy from further scorn from his peers. Will tries to explain to Marcus that nothing he does will be able to make his mom permanently happy and that he should concentrate on taking care of himself. Marcus disagrees with Will's self-protective philosophy and steps onstage, willing to be a fool in order to bring joy to his mother. Marcus starts getting heckled by his classmates, but before he can get too discouraged, Will follows his courageous example, taking a risk to help his friend.

**comfort zones, family, isolation,
reaching out, selfishness,
serving one another**

By the Book

Genesis 2:18; Psalm 133:1; Galatians 5:13; Philippians 2:4; Hebrews 3:13;
Hebrews 10:25; 1 Peter 4:8

Where to take it

- Even though the whole audience makes fun of Marcus, Will steps out of his comfort zone to help him sing a song. Have you ever done something like that for someone? Would you?

- Describe a person you know who lives as an "island." Why do you think this person chooses to be so disconnected from others?

- Watch the part of the scene before Marcus sings his song, and listen to what Will says to the boy. Is there anything that Will tells Marcus that you think holds true in life?

- Read Galatians 5:13. What does it mean to serve another person?

- Who is speaking into your life? Who is your "Will"?

Adaptation

Trailer

Who's watching out for you?

The movie comedy/drama, R

Charlie Kaufman (Nicholas Cage) is an L.A. screenwriter who has been hindered all his life by feelings of inadequacy and self-loathing. When he accepts an offer to adapt a book about flowers into a screenplay for a movie, his feelings of incompetence overwhelm him, and he gets to the point of severe writer's block. He quickly realizes that he cannot make the script interesting. Charlie's twin brother, Donald (also played by Nicholas Cage), who couldn't be more different from Charlie, decides to write a movie of his own. Donald's script is typical Hollywood fluff, which further undermines Charlie's attempt to write something meaningful. Under pressure to produce something, Charlie makes two drastic decisions: He writes himself into the screenplay and takes a trip across the county to track down the author of the original book, Susan Orlean (Meryl Streep). Both of these choices change his life forever.

This clip (about 2 1/2 minutes)

▶ **Start** / 1:35:40 / "I don't want to die, Donald. I've wasted my life. God, I've wasted it."

■ **Stop** / 1:38:00 / Scene can stop on Charlie crying.

Charlie and Donald discover far more than they bargained for when they trail Susan Orlean to Florida. When Susan learns that she is being followed and that Charlie has discovered her secret, she snaps and resolves to kill him. The two brothers get trapped in a swamp as they try to escape the crazed woman. With their lives in danger, Charlie begins to evaluate how he has lived his life. What Charlie has always viewed as weakness in his brother, he now realizes is wisdom in how to live unconstrained by self-doubt and the opinion of others.

By the Book

Psalm 71:5; 139:23-24; Ecclesiastes 7:10; Isaiah 43:18; Ecclesiastes 7:10; Galatians 1:10; 1 Timothy 4:12-16

Where to take it

- Have you ever been so embarrassed by what others said about you that it corroded your confidence? Why?

- Do you have a difficult story that made you into the person you are today?

- Which brother are you more like: Charlie, the one who worries what others think, or Donald, the one who loves even if it means looking like a fool?

- Donald's philosophy is "You are what you love, not what loves you." What does this quote mean to you?

- What is a Scripture you live by? How did it become so important to you?

- Is there anything from school that haunts you? If you could go back and make it right, how would you change what happened?

- 1 Timothy 4:12-16 is a portion of the Apostle Paul's encouragement to a much younger Timothy. How can you apply this passage to your life daily?

Almost Famous

Trailer

Have you ever been confronted about your character?

The movie — comedy, R

William Miller (Patrick Fugit) is a 15-year-old aspiring writer who loves rock 'n' roll. When his articles catch the eye of the editors at *Rolling Stone* magazine, William gets the opportunity of a lifetime—to go on the road with the up-and-coming rock band Stillwater. William's overprotective mother (Frances McDormand) is not happy, but after her daughter leaves home to escape her strict ways, Mrs. Miller reluctantly agrees to let William chase his dream. Once William joins the tour, he quickly learns that there is much more to write about than music.

This clip (just under 2 minutes)

▶ **Start** / 1:10:50 / "I'm going to fly back Monday morning."

■ **Stop** / 1:12:47 / "You know, I'm glad we spoke."

William calls home to tell his mother that he is staying on the road a few more days. One of the band members, Russell Hammond (Billy Crudup) takes the phone away from him and tries to sweet talk Mrs. Miller in an attempt to get William out of trouble. Russell's grand gesture to rescue William unwittingly lands him on the hot seat with William's mom. Russell is unable to charm her, and she quickly cuts through the sweet talk to confront Russell about his lifestyle. She challenges him to get her son home safely and to make his own life more than what it is.

By the Book

Psalm 94:12; Proverbs 17:10; Matthew 18:15-17; Romans 16:17-19; 1 Thessalonians 5:14; Titus 2:6-8; Hebrews 4:16

Where to take it

- Have you ever tried to charm someone but failed?

- Has a stranger, an acquaintance, or a friend ever confronted you about the way you live your life? Was there any truth to their accusation?

- What does Matthew 18:15-17 say about how to confront someone? Do we tend to do this or take matters into our own hands?

- William's mother tries to encourage Russell with a famous quotation: "Be bold, and mighty forces will come to your aid." How does this compare to what is written in Hebrews 4:16? What is your part, and what is God's part?

- William's mom tells Russell, "It's not too late for you to become a person of substance." What does this statement mean? Do you agree?

- Has anyone ever said something to you that changed you? What did the person say?

Antwone Fisher

The movie drama, PG-13

Antwone Fisher (Derek Luke) is on the verge of being kicked out of the Navy
because he cannot control his anger. After a fight with a man who outranks
him, Fisher is placed on restriction and sent to Dr. Jerome Davenport (Denzel
Washington) for an evaluation. Davenport doesn't allow Antwone to breeze
through their sessions; he wants to uncover the roots of the young man's
violent behavior. At first, Fisher is wary of digging up his past, but he soon
begins to trust the doctor, confiding in him the truth about the death of his
father, being abandoned by his mother, and the abuses he endured in his
foster family. At Davenport's urging, Antwone travels back to Cleveland to see
if he can find his family and get answers to some of the questions that have
kept him unsettled.

This clip (about 12 minutes)

▶ **Start** /1:38:00 / "I don't know. What do you think?"

■ **Stop** /1:50:22 / "You want some pancakes?"

After many phone calls in search of his father's family, Antwone makes contact
with his father's sister. He goes to her house and, during their conversation,
discovers that his mother is living close by. Antwone takes the opportunity to
meet her. Although he doesn't get answers to his questions about why she
walked away, he tells his mother about the man he has become and how he
has always wanted to be a part of her life. When Antwone returns to his aunt's
house, he is greeted by a number of his relatives he has never known. After a
lifetime of feeling alone and abandoned, he is finally welcomed to feast at the
table of his real family.

By the Book

Psalm 27:10; 68:5; Isaiah 49:15-16; John 1:12-13; Ephesians 6:1;
Colossians 3:20-21; Titus 2:4; 1 John 3:1; Revelation 19:7-9

Where to take it

? Antwone asks his real mother, "Why didn't you ever come for me or wonder where I was or what I was doing?" Do you think adopted children have feelings similar to Antwone's? Have you ever known anyone who was adopted? What seemed to be the biggest struggle for them?

? Read Psalm 27:10, Psalm 68:5, and Isaiah 49:15-16. What do these verses tell you about God's love and provision for those who have been forgotten by their parents?

? Describe what family means to you.

? In Colossians 3:20,21, Titus 2:4, and Ephesians 6:11, what guidelines does the Bible give us to have a healthy family?

? What do you know about the history of your family? Do you think it is important to understand your heritage? Why or why not?

? After his encounter with his mother, Antwone comes back to a house full of relatives. One of his grandmothers welcomes him to a table full of food. Read Revelation 19:7-9. What do you think the "family reunion" in heaven is going to be like? How does it make you feel to know that you have been invited to the biggest celebration of all time? Who would you most like to accompany to the feast?

Austin Powers in Goldmember

Trailer

It's so obvious. Just like the nose...
or mole on your face.

The movie comedy, PG-13

Austin Powers (Mike Myers) is the international man of mystery who, once again, is trying to thwart his nemesis, Dr. Evil (Mike Myers), who plans to destroy the world. This time, Dr. Evil has teamed up with Goldmember (Myers, again), a quirky Dutch criminal genius who has kidnapped Austin's father, Nigel Powers (Michael Caine). Austin travels back in time and lands in Goldmember's roller disco. With the help of an undercover agent, Foxxy Cleopatra (Beyonce Knowles), Austin finds his father. However, Goldmember recaptures Nigel Powers and heads back to the "present" to join the ruthless Dr. Evil in a partnership to take over the world.

This clip (just under 2 minutes)

▶ **Start** / 0:39:01 / "Awww Basil. What's happening, baby?"

■ **Stop** / 0:40:43 / "Moley, Molay, Molay, Moley."

Austin and Foxxy get a visit from Basil Exposition (Michael York) with news that one of their own agents from British intelligence has infiltrated Dr. Evil's organization. Basil introduces Austin and Foxxy to the mole (Fred Savage). Ironically, this spy, known as Number Three, has a huge mole on his face, and Austin cannot take his eyes off of the enormous protrusion as Number Three reveals information concerning the whereabouts of Dr. Evil's new lair. Although Basil and Foxxy try to keep Austin from embarrassing himself and the double agent, they fail. The mole proves to be too much for Austin, and he can't keep from blurting out various comments about it.

By the Book

1 Samuel 16:7; Psalm 139:14; John 7:24; Romans 12:2; 2 Corinthians 12:9-10;
Galatians 6:3,7

Where to take it

(?) Name three attributes you like about
yourself.

(?) Name one thing about yourself you
wish were different. Would you
change this feature if you had the
opportunity? Why or why not?

(?) Do you get caught up in what you look
like and what you wear?

(?) Too often we concentrate on external
qualities rather than internal ones. Why
do you think our society emphasizes
outward appearances? How much value do you
put on external appearances?

(?) If friends and family were to name one character weakness in your life,
what do you think they'd say?

(?) If we have character weaknesses that are obvious to others, why do you
think we still focus our attention on changing our external appearances
rather than transforming our internal characteristics?

(?) What does the Bible have to say about outward appearances versus
internal character?

Bedazzled

Trailer

The devil will try to confuse you.

The movie   comedy, PG-13

Elliot Richard (Brendan Fraser) is a computer nerd who, try as he might, cannot get woman to like him. He has a longtime crush on a coworker, and when she brushes him off, too, he vows to do anything to make her a part of his life. That's when the devil (Elizabeth Hurley) makes her entrance. In exchange for his soul, Elliot can have seven wishes to create any life he wants. He requests everything he has ever dreamed of, but none of his scenarios turn out the way he envisioned. The devil always throws in a twist, leaving him unsatisfied. Elliot finds that life isn't so grand on the other side of the fence and wants a chance to get it right with the life he originally had. The devil, however, wants her due and has no plans to let Elliot go without a fight.

This clip   (just under 2 minutes)

▶ **Start** / 1:14:12 / "I sold my soul."

■ **Stop** / 1:16:00 / Elliot shakes his head as scene fades.

When Elliot refuses to make his seventh wish to seal the deal, he finds himself arrested and thrown in jail by none other than the devil posing as a cop. His mysterious cellmate takes the opportunity to talk with Elliot about his predicament, and this prisoner seems to be able to see a reality beyond what the devil has convinced Elliot is true. Talking to Elliot about the devil's tactics, the mysterious cellmate encourages him to see who really holds the fate of his soul.

By the Book

Psalm 25:1; Ezekiel 18:4; Matthew 16:26; 2 Corinthians 11:13-15; 1 Peter 5:8

Where to take it

(?) Has there ever been a time when you felt as if you sold out to something or someone even though you knew it wasn't right? Did you suffer any consequences?

(?) The mysterious cellmate says, "Your soul doesn't belong to you, it belongs to God." Do you feel this is true? Do you act as if this is true? Is this true? Read Ezekiel 18:4. What does this say about our souls?

(?) Read 2 Corinthians 11:13-15. How does the devil try to confuse you?

(?) His cellmate tells Elliot, "In the end, you're going to see clearly who and what you are and what you are here to do." To the group, describe who you are. What do you think God's purpose is for your life?

(?) Describe Satan in your own words. Now, read how 1 Peter 5:8 describes Satan. Does your view match up to God's Word?

(?) How do you think Satan tries to deceive you? Can you describe a time when you knew there was a spiritual battle going on? How did you respond?

The Best Bits of Mr. Bean

Trailer

Is church boring you to sleep?

The movie — comedy, Not Rated

Mr. Bean (Rowan Atkinson) is the king of saying nothing and yet saying so much. In this collection of mini-vignettes, Mr. Bean gets ready for work in the car, goes to the dentist, dives off the tallest diving board, and cooks a Thanksgiving turkey. This lovable misfit causes the most outrageous predicaments, and the viewer cannot help but enjoy the outlandish outcomes. Pulling his trademark faces, Rowan Atkinson makes fun of every situation that Mr. Bean encounters.

This clip (about 9 minutes)

- ▶ **Start** / 0:43:50 / Mr. Bean drives up to church and backs into a car.

- ■ **Stop** / 0:53:10 / Mr. Bean puts jelly bean into "snotty" pocket.

Although Mr. Bean wants to enjoy a church service, he cannot seem to stay awake. He makes his best attempts to stay alert, trying not to bother the churchgoers sitting next to him. Mr. Bean also tries to sing the hymns without knowing the words, does his best to thwart a sneeze, and fumbles his way through the sometimes mundane "rituals" of church. Although no words are spoken by this modern-day Charlie Chaplin, he communicates a lot as he makes us think about how sometimes we, too, just try to get through church Sunday after Sunday.

By the Book

Psalm 5:7; 33:1; 35:18; 100:4; Romans 12:4-21; 1 Corinthians 12:28; Hebrews 10:24,25

Where to take it

(?) While everything in a church service could be so interesting, why does it sometimes seem so dull and boring?

(?) Why do you think some churches avoid alternate types of worship such as "contemporary" music in their services? Should poetry, band instruments, drama, painting, etc., be allowed in church services? Why or why not?

(?) Do you think that any type of church service has its place as long as God is glorified? Is there any type of church service that shouldn't be used, even if it glorifies God? Why or why not?

(?) Romans 12:4-21 has a lot to say about how we should conduct ourselves and how we should "do church." As you read these verses, what is emphasized?

(?) Why do you go to church? What do you think is the purpose of the church?

(?) Do you try just to make it through church on Sunday morning, or do you make an effort to engage in the service, discovering what you can?

(?) What helps you connect with God and learn more about him?

Big Fat Liar

Trailer

Does lying work for you?

The movie   comedy, PG

Jason Shepherd (Frankie Muniez) is a grand storyteller. Because he has told so many stories to get himself out of trouble, he has a hard time telling anything that is true. For class, he can't stick to any truth no matter what because he is usually making up stories to get himself out of trouble. Jason writes a class paper called "Big Fat Liar," and on his way to deliver it to his teacher, he crosses paths with Marty Wolf (Paul Giamatti), a sleazy Hollywood producer who is an even bigger liar than Jason. Marty steals the paper, which gets Jason into more trouble with his parents and lands him in summer school. Jason's parents don't believe his claim that his paper was stolen because he has crossed the line dividing fact and fiction too many times. Jason decides to take a trip to Tinseltown in order to redeem himself by retrieving his work and getting Marty to admit what he has done.

This clip   (just under 4 minutes)

▶ **Start** / 0:02:16 / "Ms. Caldwell? Can you open the door? It's kinda toasty in here."

■ **Stop** / 0:06:12 / "That should be no problem since making up stories seems to be your God-given talent."

Jason is having a rough morning. He gets to school late and is locked out, so he attempts to sneak into his classroom through the window and join in the discussion without the teacher noticing. When she asks him to read his assignment, he begins to spin a tale and cover his tracks. But as clever as he is, he gets caught and must write the paper in three hours or fail the class.

By the Book

Psalm 51:6; Proverbs 19:5; John 8:32; 1 Peter 3:10

Where to take it

- Discuss a time when a lie seemed like a good alternative to the truth. Do you still feel that way?

- Can you remember any of the "stories" you have told that may have grown so big that you couldn't keep the lies straight? What were the consequences of your "story"?

- Is there ever a good reason to withhold the truth? Have you learned any lessons from telling only parts of the truth? What discourages you from telling the whole truth?

- Have you ever found yourself in a more difficult situation because you told the truth?

- In John 8:32, Jesus says that the truth will set you free. What do you think he means?

- Have you ever had the the reputation of a liar? What, if anything, did you do to try to change that?

The Big Kahuna

Trailer

When is talking about Jesus a "no-no"?

The movie   drama, R

Larry (Kevin Spacey) and Phil (Danny Devito) are longtime sales partners who are travelling with a rookie, Bob (Peter Facinelli), to their industry's convention in Wichita, Kansas. Foremost on Larry's and Phil's minds is to land an account with a man they call "The Big Kahuna," otherwise known as Mr. Fuller, who is the president of a major corporation. Getting his business would mean substantial revenue for the company. However, there is more than selling going on between these men. By the end of the convention, their lives and their conflicting ideas about their jobs may be bigger obstacles to overcome than trying to land a deal with "El Kahuna Grande."

This clip   (just under 8 minutes)

▶ **Start** / 1:08:43 / "Oh, he's here. I told you."

■ **Stop** / 1:16:27 / "With or without the account, we'll live."

Bob comes back to the hotel to tell Phil and Larry about his meeting with Mr. Fuller. When Bob tells Larry and Phil that he didn't talk to Mr. Fuller about industrial lubricants but talked to him about Jesus, Larry asks if Bob discussed a business deal at any point in the conversation. Bob tells him that he thought it would be insincere if he brought up business once he and Mr. Fuller had been discussing matters of faith. Larry accuses Bob of being just as deceitful by claiming that his sole purpose for the conversation with Mr. Fuller was to preach Christ.

Additional clip   (just under 5 minutes)

▶ **Start** / 1:19:58 / Phil lights a cigarette.

■ **Stop** / 1:24:47 / Phil finishes his discussion with Bob.

TIP: You can forward the movie to another segment where Phil talks to Bob about honesty, character, and what he thinks it means to truly "witness" to someone (approx. 5 more minutes of footage; start at 1:19:58 – stop at 1:24:47).

42

By the Book

Matthew 28:19; Acts 22:15; Colossians 3:17; 1 Timothy 1:5; Hebrews 4:12

Where to take it

- ❓ Are there any instances when sharing Christ with someone is inappropriate? If so, what are those times?

- ❓ Larry tells Bob that, even though he understands that the young man has a strong desire to share what he believes, the way he handled the conversation was just as insincere as if he had been talking to Mr. Fuller only because he wanted to sell him a product. Do you agree or disagree?

- ❓ Do non-Christians think the same way Larry does—that most Christians want to "sell" Jesus instead of getting to know people before witnessing to them?

- ❓ Do you think that there is a right way and/or a wrong way to talk about Christ with someone?

- ❓ Larry gets upset when Bob tries to quote Scripture. Larry says that he wasn't there with Jesus, so he doesn't know what was said, arguing that the Bible is a book a bunch of people wrote and passed down. How do you feel about this?

- ❓ Read Matthew 28:19, Colossians 3:17, and Hebrews 4:12. What does the Bible say about witnessing? About Scripture? About living our lives as believers in an unbelieving world?

Trailer

Are you headed for "big trouble"?

The movie   comedy, PG-13

What could possibly bring together the lives of a divorced dad, the son who doesn't respect him, two determined hit men, a couple of brainless thugs, a pair of FBI agents, one hard-working cop, her bumbling partner, a moody housewife, her daughter, her detestable husband, and one very cranky toad? It could only be a silver case containing a contraption that looks like a garbage disposal but is actually a nuclear bomb. Snake Dupree (Tom Sizemore) and Eddie Ledbetter (Johnny Knoxville) are the two brainless thugs who decide to rob a bar that is actually a front for a weapons dealer. Finding no money in the cash register, they take the silver case, unaware that it is a bomb, and instead believe what is inside will lead them to a big payoff. In their efforts to get all they can and leave the country, they end up involving numerous people in the chaos of their journey to bigger and better things.

This clip   (about 2 minutes)

▶ **Start** / 1:12:43 / "Get the suitcase off the plane...the suitcase...get it off the plane!"

■ **Stop** / 1:14:40 / Scene ends with mushroom cloud over the sea.

Snake and Eddie manage to get the silver case onto a small plane bound for the Bahamas. While attempting to get the case through security, Snake unknowingly activates the timer on the bomb. Eliot Arnold (Tim Allen) chases down the plane as it taxis away from the gate, and he sneaks onboard in order to rescue his son's friend, who has been taken hostage. When the pilots get word from the FBI that there is a bomb in the silver case, it is Eliot's responsibility to get it off the plane. Snake is determined not to let go of what he is convinced is his ticket to the "good life."

By the Book

Proverbs 14:12; Matthew 6:24; Mark 8:36; Colossians 3:5

Where to take it

? In a humorous visual, we see everyone trying to get the bomb off the plane. Then Snake jumps after the bomb into the open air. Have you ever jumped into a dangerous situation without thinking or caring that it might be bad for you?

? Eliot tries to help Snake back into the plane, telling him to let go of the case. Describe a time when someone told you to let go of something that was harming you or others in your life, but you held on to it and wouldn't let go.

? At one point, Snake is hanging on to both the case (that could destroy him) and the plane (that could save him). Have you ever tried to hang on to something that could hurt you and something that could help you at the same time?

? What do you hold onto rather than give over to God? Is there any benefit to holding on? Have you suffered any consequences for holding on too tightly?

45

Who are you…really?

The movie   drama, PG-13

Frank Abagnale (Leonardo DiCaprio) runs away from home after he learns that his parents are getting a divorce. Believing that financial problems are at the root of his family's demise, Abagnale is determined to fix everything by achieving the success that eluded his father. On his own, he quickly figures out how to pass himself off as an airline pilot, and by developing his check-forging abilities, he rewards himself with a handsome "salary." When Abagnale's illegal activity is noticed by FBI agent Carl Hanratty (Tom Hanks), the chase is on. Determined to track down the criminal, Hanratty trails him all over the world, but every time he gets close, Abagnale is one step ahead of him. Along the way, the two men develop an interesting relationship that goes beyond "cat and mouse" and becomes a friendship.

This clip   (about 1 minute)

▶ **Start** / 0:3:03 / "Based on a true story."

■ **Stop** / 0:04:41/ "His name was Carl Hanratty."

Three men in pilots' uniforms walk onstage, all claiming to be Frank William Abagnale, Jr. They are on the game show, *To Tell the Truth*, and the announcer gives some background of Abagnale's stints as an airline pilot, doctor, and lawyer—all pulled off before he was 18 years old. The contestants then question the three gentlemen about the life of the infamous con man in order to make the best guess as to which of them is the real Frank Abagnale.

By the Book

Psalm 101:7; Proverbs 19:5; Matthew 25:14-30; Romans 11:29;
1 Corinthians 14:12; Colossians 3:17; 1 Peter 3:10

Where to take it

? Do you think Frank Abagnale should have been proud of the many ways he became an imposter, or should he have been ashamed of them? Who do you think was hurt by Frank's lies?

? If your life was put on display and you had to "tell the truth," what would the audience discover about you? Of what are you most proud in your life so far? What do you most regret?

? A contestant asks one of the men posing as Abagnale why, if he was so bright and talented, he chose to use his talents to deceive. Have you ever known someone who was very talented but just didn't use his or her gifts in the right way? What are your gifts and talents? How are you planning to use them in your life?

? What is your response to this saying: "Our talents are a gift from God, and what we do with those talents is our gift back to God"?

? Do you use any of your skills, talents, and/or intelligence for the wrong reasons? Is there a payoff for misusing them?

? In what ways or areas are you an impostor? How are you trying to fool the people around you?

? In Matthew 25:14-30, what does Jesus say will happen if our talents are not used for God's glory?

Changing Lanes

Trailer

By what standards do you live?

The movie   drama, R

Gavin Banek (Ben Affleck) is a corporate attorney for a high-power firm. Doyle Gipson (Samuel L. Jackson) is a recovering alcoholic trying to get his life and family back on track. On a rainy Good Friday in New York, their two cars collide on a busy freeway. Because Gavin is in a hurry to get to court for an important case, he doesn't offer Doyle insurance information or a ride, leaving him with his wrecked car. Stranded, Doyle misses his appointment at court to fight for custody of his two children. When Gavin gets to the courthouse for his case, he realizes that he left a key document at the scene of the accident, and Doyle has it. Once Doyle realizes what he has, the two become locked in a battle of wills that swiftly escalates, and they become intent on destroying each other.

This clip   (about 6 minutes)

▶ **Start** / 1:23:22 / "Come on, how do you think Simon Dunn got his money?"

■ **Stop** / 1:29:34 / "Me too."

Gavin is tormented by guilt for his involvement in a fraudulent deal with an elderly client. His client was too sick to know the consequences of signing over control of his money over to Gavin's firm. Prepared to go to the authorities to confess his wrongdoing, he reveals his plans to come clean to his boss (Sidney Pollack). However, he learns that the loose ends have already been tied up by the other partners in the firm, and Gavin's boss explains how he justified his actions. When Gavin goes back to his office, he finds Doyle waiting for him. Doyle has returned the missing file and wants to call a truce. The two men discuss what the day has taught them about their lives and their characters. Finally, they seek forgiveness from one another.

By the Book

Proverbs 16:18; Romans 3:24; 12:2,17-18; Galatians 5:19-21;
Ephesians 2:8; 4:26; 1 John 2:16

Where to take it

- Gavin's boss says he can live with himself because, at the end of the day, he believes he does more good than harm. What do you think of his philosophy? Read Romans 3:24 and Ephesians 2:8. What do these passages say about this type of balancing act?

- Gavin's boss asks him, "What other standard have I got to judge by?" Read Romans 12:2 and Galatians 5:19-21. What would you say to him about God's standards and morality?

- Gavin talks about a day on a beach and making a choice. Describe a time when you were faced with a choice to make that you knew could change your future.

- Tell the group about a time when you crossed paths with someone, and it changed the course of your life.

- The last three lines of a Robert Frost's poem "The Road Not Taken" are, "Two roads diverged in a wood/And I took the one less traveled by/and that has made all the difference." What does this mean to you?

- Gavin and Doyle tell each other they are sorry for their actions that day. Do you find apologizing easy? Why or why not?

- Why can we say we are "sorry" for so many little things (e.g., dropping or spilling something), but when it comes to matters of the heart, "sorry" can be the most difficult word to say?

- Read 1 John 2:16. How does pride keep us from truly living our lives for God?

Clockstoppers

Trailer

What if you could stop time for just
one day of your life?

The movie   comedy/sci-fi, PG

Zak Gibbs (Jesse Bradford) is a high-school kid anxious to put a down payment
on his first car, but he can't get his dad (Robin Thomas) away from his work
long enough to take him to the car lot. What Zak doesn't know is that his dad
is helping develop a device that speeds up the molecules of a person so quickly
that the rest of the world seems frozen in time around him. Such a device is
exactly what the power-hungry leader of the development project wants
under his control. The government knows about the project and orders it to
be halted so that the technology doesn't fall into the wrong hands. When Zak
finds the watch and learns how to use it, he gets himself involved in the
adventure of his life.

This clip   (about 2 minutes)

▶ **Start** / 0:32:57 / "Well...with such awesome power
comes awesome responsibility."

⏹ **Stop** / 0:35:01 / Policewoman shoos a dog out of car
she is writing a ticket for.

Zak first discovers the watch's potential at his friend Francesca's (Paula Garces)
house. After testing it in her backyard and realizing they have the power to
alter their environment and the people in it, the two set out to see what they
can accomplish. They enter into a number of situations and choose to
manipulate them; then they stand back and watch their work unfold.

50

By the Book

Genesis 50:20; 1 Chronicles 29:11; Romans 8:28; Philippians 3:13-14

Where to take it

? If you could turn back time, what would you want to re-do? Would you use the power to help others or use it for your own benefit?

? What are some of the things you'd do right away if you had a watch or some type of contraption that could stop time? Do you think you would bend the rules a little with this new-found power? How hard would it be to keep from getting yourself into some type of trouble with a power like this?

? What are the pros and cons of a technology like hyper time?

? Name some ways in your world (and in the world as a whole) that people with power have used it for good purposes and/or wrong purposes.

Trailer

Does God give justice?

The movie   drama, PG-13

Edmond Dantes (Jim Caviezel) is young sailor with a strong character and noble spirit who is betrayed by his best friend, Fernand Mondego (Guy Piearce). Fernand is fueled by intense envy, and he's especially envious of Edmond because of his beautiful fiancée, Mercedes (Dagmarya Dominczyk). Fernand uses a naïve mistake that Edmond makes to orchestrate a false accusation of treason that sends Dantes to the torturous island prison, Chateau d'If. There he meets Abbé Faria (Richard Harris), or "Priest" as Edmond calls him, and the two men join forces to escape. In the process, Edmond learns to read, write, and fight. He also comes to understand the depth of the deception that brought him to prison and the keys to setting things right when he again meets his betrayers face to face.

This clip   (12 minutes)

▶ **Start** / 0:27:45 / Edmond walks up the prison steps.

■ **Stop** / 0:39:45 / "Revenge."

Edmond enters the prison believing that those responsible for putting him there will come to recognize his innocence. When he is led to his cell, he sees an inscription on the wall: "God will give me justice." Edmond clings to that hope, inscribing the letters deeper into the stones. Gradually, his hope and his conviction fade, as God seems intent on keeping silent and his suffering does not end. The cruelty of the prison embitters Edmond toward the God he believed would vindicate him. His thoughts of faith and love change to thoughts of anger and vengeance toward those who betrayed his name and his character.

By the Book

Deuteronomy 20:4; 1 Samuel 17:47; Job 1:13-22; Isaiah 35:4; 40:31;
Matthew 27:27-44; Acts 16:22-25; Romans 12:19; 1 Peter 2:19

Where to take it

? When Edmond says that God has faded from his heart, Priest asks him what replaced God. Discuss a time in your life when something "replaced" the love of God in your heart.

? Have you ever been wrongly accused or punished for a long period of time before you felt God rescued you? Why do you think it took so long? What are the lessons you learned from that period of life?

? We see Edmond falter from strong faith to weak faith to almost unbelief. Have you ever experienced a change in how much faith you had in God and his promises?

? Is it hard to remain a strong believer when you are being persecuted and mocked? Read Acts 16:22-25. How did Paul and Silas respond to their persecution?

? Read Job 1:13-22. How did Job respond to God after losing everything?

? Read Matthew 27:27-44. What was the extent of Jesus' pain and persecution? How does reading about Jesus' pain and suffering make you feel when you compare it to your own?

? Do you think God answers the question, "Why me?" What questions do you ask God when you are facing difficult circumstances, pain, loss, and betrayal?

Do you feel like a "mistake"?

The movie   drama, PG-13

Three childhood friends, Lucy (Britney Spears), Kit (Zoe Saldana), and Mimi (Taryn Manning), bury a box containing items that symbolize their dreams. They pledge to dig up the box on the night of their high-school graduation. Years later, as they are unearthing the container, Lucy, Mimi, and Kit realize that not only have their friendships turned out differently from what they expected but also their lives are far short of what they had hoped they would be. So the girls decide to embark on a road trip to pursue the dreams they once had.

This clip   (about 6 minutes)

▶ **Start** / 0:59:00 / Vintage car pulls up to house.

■ **Stop** / 1:05:00 / "You have us."

Lucy's dream is to find the mother (Kim Cattrall) who abandoned her when she was young. Lucy's dad (Dan Aykroyd) has never allowed her to try to contact her mother. Deciding to make the trip to Arizona for what she is convinced will be a warm reunion with her mother, Lucy is disappointed and finds that her mother wants nothing to do with her. Though brokenhearted, Lucy does discover another "family"—her friends.

By the Book

Psalm 139:14; 68:5-6; 27:10; Isaiah 49:15-16; Matthew 7:11; John 1:12-13;
1 John 3:1

Where to take it

(?) Lucy tries to reconnect with her mom who clearly does not want Lucy to be a part of her life. Can you identify with how she must feel?

(?) Finish this sentence: "The ideal family is _____."

(?) John 1:12-13 talks about being adopted into God's family. How would you describe to Lucy what this means?

(?) In the clip, Lucy believes she was a "mistake." Have you ever felt like this? Do you think it is possible for people who feel like a mistake to overcome this feeling?

(?) Read Psalm 27:10 and Isaiah 49:15-16. How do these verses relate to Lucy? How do they apply to you?

(?) Describe the parent you hope to be someday.

Disney's The Kid

Trailer

How well do you know your "inner kid"?

The movie   comedy, PG

Russ Duritz (Bruce Willis) is a highly successful image consultant. He's a brazen and merciless man who shows no emotion, can't tolerate people who do, has no time for family or friends, and thrives in his job telling people what to do and how to live. Two days before his 40th birthday, he gets a visit from Rusty (Spencer Breslin), the eight-year-old version of himself. Neither Russ nor Rusty is thrilled with the meeting—or with the other version of himself. Rusty is a chubby, curious, playful little boy who reminds Russ of everything he has tried to repress or change. Rusty is upset that Russ doesn't grow up to be anything he wanted to be: he doesn't have a dog, a wife, or kids. Rusty thinks Russ is a total loser. Together, the pair must figure out the meaning of their encounter and, more importantly, the purpose of their lives.

This clip (about 3 minutes)

▶ **Start** / 1:27:03 / "Look, Daddy's home."

■ **Stop** / 1:30:05 / "OK, but I'm eating whatever I want."

Convinced one event on the playground is the turning point in his life, Russ travels back to his childhood with Rusty, hoping to confront that event. He is wrong. The real defining moment happens later that day. When Rusty's dad (Daniel Von Bargen) finds out that his wife had to leave the house to get Rusty at school, he becomes enraged. Driven by his own anxiety and pain, the father lashes out at Rusty, telling him that his mother is dying, so he needs to quit crying and be a man. As Russ watches the scene, he realizes the impact this moment has had on his life and tries to explain it to Rusty. Russ tells his younger self that his father is not angry with Rusty, but is afraid of losing his wife and raising the family on his own.

By the Book

Proverbs 22:6; Ecclesiastes 11:9-10; Matthew 6:14; Luke 11:13;
1 Corinthians 13:11; Ephesians 4:14-15; 6:4; Hebrews 13:7

Where to take it

? What words or events from childhood still impact you today?

? Share with the group (or with someone you can confide in) painful memories you have held inside.

? Does something your parents said still linger in your mind? What may be a result of that memory?

? If you could fast-forward your life 20 years from today, what character traits might you see in yourself as a result of a childhood incident?

? What do you think it means when people say God can be our heavenly father? Is this a hard concept for you to grasp? Why?

? In this scene, Russ gets a chance to look back and see that his dad's cruelty was caused by his fear. Have there been moments in your life when your parents may have reacted out of fear? How does understanding this help you overcome the pain now?

? Do you see any of your own parents' attitudes or behaviors developing in you? What are some of the positive ones?

The Divine Secrets of the Ya-Ya Sisterhood

Trailer

Do you keep praying for "more"?

The movie   comedy, PG-13

Siddalee Walker (Sandra Bullock) has never seen eye to eye with her mother, Vivi (Ellen Burstyn). Even though they now live miles apart, Sidda and her mother still have trouble keeping their relationship civil. Things change when an article about Sidda appears in *Time* magazine. The reporter prints only a portion of Sidda's comments about her childhood, inferring that Vivi was not a good mother. Vivi is infuriated, and an even bigger chasm develops between the two. Vivi's lifelong friends, known as the Ya-Ya Sisterhood, take it upon themselves to reconcile mother and daughter; they kidnap Sidda and take her back to where she grew up in Louisiana. As the Ya-Yas divulge all the secrets of their lives, Sidda comes to understand why her mother is the way she is. Eventually, Sidda begins to forgive and accept her complicated and temperamental mother.

This clip   (about 4 minutes)

▶ **Start** / 1:42:15 / Sidda walks over to her mother and sits besides her.

■ **Stop** / 1:46:30 / Mother and daughter hug.

Having been released by her Ya-Ya captors, Sidda returns to her childhood home on her mother's birthday with a new perspective on many of the more difficult events from their past together. The two sit on the front-porch swing to talk, both ready to forgive one another and start over. Vivi takes the opportunity to tell Sidda about her new understanding of what she did wrong as a mother as well as about her perceptions of and feelings for her daughter.

By the Book

Psalm 103:12; Matthew 6:14-15; Romans 8:35-39; 1 John 1:9

Where to take it

- **(?)** Discuss a time when you asked for someone's forgiveness. What reaction did you get?

- **(?)** In this clip, Vivi claims she always kept praying for "more." Are you always asking for "more," perceiving God as a genie?

- **(?)** At one point in the clip, it is said that sometimes God answers prayers, but we miss it. The blessings and the answers are with us all along, but we keep looking elsewhere. Is there an area of your life where this may be the case?

- **(?)** As the mother talks about forgiveness, she states, "There are things for which I don't expect to be forgiven…not even by God." What do you think about this statement?

- **(?)** What is the difference between beating yourself up for your past actions and experiencing the consequences of your actions?

- **(?)** What does it mean to reconcile? Are there any relationships in your life that need to be reconciled? What about your relationship with God?

Dragonfly

Is suicide a sin?

The movie drama, PG-13

Dr. Joe Darrow's (Kevin Costner) wife, Emily (Susanna Thompson), dies in a bus crash while working with the Red Cross in South America. Emily's body can't be found, and the fact that Joe doesn't know what her last moments were like haunts him. Joe's heartbreak swiftly turns into bitterness. He tries to cope with his loss by working around the clock in the hospital emergency room. A series of events and encounters begin to change Joe's beliefs about what happens after we die. And incredibly, he senses that his wife may be trying to communicate with him from beyond the grave.

This clip (under 2 minutes)

▶ **Start** / 0:0: 7:48 / "Why did you do this to me?"

■ **Stop** / 0:0: 9:09 / "Hi Father, time for a rebuttal?"

On the day of his wife's memorial service, Joe answers a page from the hospital and reports for work at the ER. While assessing patients from an auto accident, a young woman (Liza Weil) who has attempted suicide is brought to him. Joe reassigns her to another doctor because he has no compassion for a patient who has no will to live. After his shift, Joe goes to her room to check on her. During their brief conversation, Joe explains to the girl that the "better place" she is looking for does not exist.

By the Book

Deuteronomy 32:39; Matthew 5:21; John 5:24; 1 Thessalonians 4:13;
Hebrews 11:1

Where to take it

? In this clip, the suicidal girl tells Joe that no one knows her heart. Do you
ever feel like that?

? If you could tell people three of the deepest things in your heart, what
would they be?

? Is suicide wrong in the eyes of God?
Does the Bible have anything to say
about suicide?

? Describe your perception of heaven.

? In the clip, Dr. Darrow tells his
patient that she'd better be sure she's
going to a better place because, as
bad as this world is, it's all there is.
What do you think the priest who
came to visit might have said to her?
If you were called in to counsel her,
what would you say?

We are all parts of one body...
one sound.

The movie comedy, PG-13

Devon Miles (Nick Cannon) is a snare drummer who has just been granted a full scholarship to the renowned marching band at Atlanta A&T University. Although the program requires that its students sight-read music, Devon can't, so he disregards the rules and lies on his application and in his audition. Because he can replicate any piece he hears, he is confident that his talent will be enough. Devon is able to fool everyone and even makes the drumline. Soon, though, his arrogance gets the best of him, and the band director, Dr. Lee (Orlando Jones), removes him from the band, making it clear to Devon that what hinders him has nothing to do with his talent but his ability to learn and be led. Devon resists the discipline until he realizes all he might lose if he doesn't do what it takes to become a better man.

This clip (just under 4 minutes)

▶ **Start** / 0:10:38 / "When the Saints Go Marching In" cadence playing.

■ **Stop** / 0:14:27 / "That's why we're the most important section of this band."

The first morning at Atlanta A&T training camp is a rough one. Dr. Lee sends his section leaders to awaken the new freshmen before sunrise, introducing them to what it takes to achieve his vision of one band, one sound. An arrogant Devon gets his first lesson that being a part of this band is not about what he wants and what his talents are. The different instrument teams gather together, and the section leaders explain to their members the importance of the parts they will play in the band.

By the Book

Romans 12:4-13; 1 Corinthians 12:12-20,25-31; Galatians 5:13-14; 6:2; Ephesians 4:15-16; Philippians 2:3-4; James 3:16

Where to take it

(?) In this clip, Dr. Lee challenges Devon because he didn't look out for his roommate. Read 1 Corinthians 12:25-26, Galatians 5:13-14, and Galatians 6:2. What does God have to say about our responsibility to each other?

(?) The section leaders explain what makes them the important part of the band. The role each leader highlights, however, is different from the others (the trumpets are the voice; the tubas are the boom; the drums are the pulse). Read 1 Corinthians 12:12-20. What do these verses say about the importance of each part in the body of Christ?

(?) Read Romans 12:4-13 and 1 Corinthians 12:27-31, which list the different parts of the body of Christ. How do these parts of the body work together?

(?) What part(s) of the body of Christ do you feel you represent?

(?) What part(s) of the body of Christ do you feel your youth group or church best represents?

(?) What are some parts of the body of Christ listed in 1 Corinthians 12:27-31 that are seldom seen today? Refer to your list of different parts of the body. Which ones may not be utilized in your church? Why do you think this is?

The Emporer's Club

Trailer

Character will cost.

The movie drama, PG-13

Mr. Hundert (Kevin Kline) teaches Western Civilization at St. Benedict's Academy for Boys. Wanting to do more than educate his students about the ancient Greek and Roman cultures, Mr. Hundert makes every effort to mold his students into men of character, inspiring them to strive for greatness in their lives. When a troubled and disrespectful Sedgewick Bell (Emile Hirsch) arrives at the school, he tests the boundaries of Mr. Hundert's patience. Although this young man is difficult to reach, Mr. Hundert believes in him and even bends the rules to get him into the final round of the school's coveted Julius Caesar competition. Sedgewick actually wants to do well, but under the pressure, he chooses to cheat. Many years later, Mr. Hundert gets the opportunity to revisit the choices he made and reconsider the role he has played in the lives of the young men entrusted to his care.

This clip (about 2 minutes)

▶ **Start** / 0:07:55 / "You, sir. Will you do me a favor and walk to the back of this classroom...."

■ **Stop** / 0:10:12/ "Welcome to Western Civilization: The Greeks and the Romans."

Mr. Hundert begins his class by having a student read a plaque on the wall that notes the achievement of a man who lived in 1100 B.C. He asks his students to find this person in their history books, but he is not there. After explaining that no matter how successful one may think he is, if he contributes nothing to the world, he will leave no lasting legacy, Mr. Hundert also explains to his students why the names and ideas of the men they will be studying have survived over time. Then he challenges the young men to consider what they will give to the world.

By the Book

Isaiah 66:22; Matthew 25:23; Galatians 2:20; 2 Timothy 4:5; Titus 2:7-8

Where to take it

? Mr. Hundert tells his students, "Great ambition and conquest without contribution is without significance." What do you think this means?

? Of all the great men of history referred to in this clip, why do you think Jesus Christ is not mentioned as a man who made a significant contribution?

? Read Titus 2:7-8. How does this passage say we should live our lives?

? Mr. Hundert poses this question to the young men in his class: "What will your contribution be?" What do you want your legacy to be? As you look over your life, what contributions do you feel you have made so far?

? Read Matthew 25:23. What are the "few things" that God has given you to do? How are you being faithful in that regard?

? When you make a contribution that benefits others, do you prefer not to get credit or do you like to be recognized? Why?

Eye for an Eye

Trailer

Is the biblical phrase "an eye for an eye" relevant today?

The movie — thriller/drama, R

Karen McCann (Sally Field), her second husband, Mack (Ed Harris), and their two daughters lead a happy life until one day when Karen calls home to check on the preparations for their youngest daughter's birthday party. While she is talking to her older daughter, Julie (Oliva Burnette), on the phone, a stranger knocks on the door. As soon as the daughter opens the door, she is violently beaten and murdered as Karen listens to the entire event on the phone line. The killer, Robert Doob (Keifer Sutherland), is soon caught, but through a legal technicality, the charges are dropped, and he is set free. Karen and Mack attempt to put the pieces of their shattered world back together and press on for the sake of their youngest daughter, Megan (Alexandria Kyle). Still reeling and overwhelmed with grief and anger, Karen decides she wants justice and follows Robert, trying to find the best place and time to avenge her daughter's murder. Her journey leads her face to face with the killer, and she must make a choice: wait for justice from God or avenge her daughter's murder herself.

This clip (just under 1 minute)

▶ **Start** / 1:15:45 / "I was in those meetings investigating vigilante activity. I work undercover. I'm with the FBI."

■ **Stop** / 1:17:12 / Karen McCann walks down steps to gate.

Karen goes to the house of Angel Kosinsky (Charlayne Woodard), a woman she met at a support group for people who have lost loved ones to violent crime. Karen is shocked when the young man who answers the door is the same son Angel told her had been murdered. Karen discovers that her friend is really an undercover FBI agent who has been investigating people in the grief group. Angel warns Karen to stop following her daughter's killer and to leave matters in the hands of the authorities. She also confronts Karen about the kind of legacy she is leaving for Megan.

By the Book

Leviticus 19:18; 24:19-20; Ecclesiastes 3:3; Isaiah 35:4;
Matthew 5:38-39; 10:28; Romans 12:19; Titus 2:7-8

Where to take it

? Have you ever wanted to get revenge? Describe the circumstances and the emotions you experienced.

? What do you think you would you do if an intruder took the life of someone you loved?

? Read Leviticus 24:19-20. Does this apply in the world we live in today?

? Do you believe in "an eye for an eye"?

? What characteristics would people see if they watched your actions?

? Describe the kind of legacy you want to leave.

? What did your parents teach you about right and wrong?

? When you're a parent, what will you teach your children about the most important virtues of life?

? Read Leviticus 19:18 and Ecclesiastes 3:3 from the Old Testament and Matthew 5:38-39 and Romans 12:19 from the New Testament. In what ways do the Old and New Testaments differ about taking matters of vengeance into your own hands?

Far from Heaven

Should homosexuality
be kept a secret?

The movie   drama, PG-13

Frank (Dennis Quaid) and Catherine Whitaker (Julianne Moore) have the typical 1950s suburban family…or do they? Frank, a top executive at a mega-electronics company, is struggling with and repulsed by his longing for men. Catherine, the darling girl of the Hartford community who always does what is expected of her, can't talk to her high-society friends about her troubled marriage, so she turns to her gardener (Dennis Haysbert) for comfort and companionship. This causes a stir in the town because he is also a black man. It is only a matter of time before this "ideal" family and the bubble they live in bursts as a result of bigotry, secrets, and pain.

This clip (about 5 minutes)

▶ **Start** / 0:26:11 / "Mr. Maynard…left an estimate for the roof."

■ **Stop** / 0:31:33 / "So help me God."

Catherine discovers Frank with another man when she brings her husband some dinner at work. Frank comes home later that night to an utterly stunned and confused wife, and he tells her that he is going to find a doctor who can help him. Dutifully, Catherine goes with Frank to see a doctor. Although the doctor's outlook is not terribly encouraging, Frank is convinced that he will beat his attraction to men because he does not want to ruin his family.

By the Book

Leviticus 18:22; 20:13; Romans 1:26-28; 1 Corinthians 10:13;
1 Thessalonians 4:3; Hebrews 2:18; 4:15

Where to take it

(?) In your opinion, is homosexuality something people are born with or is it a choice?

(?) Do you know anyone who is struggling with homosexuality? What are his or her biggest fears? What does that person wish people knew about what he or she is going through?

(?) Read Leviticus 18:22, Leviticus 20:13, and Romans 1:26-28. What do these passages say about homosexuality? In what ways does our current culture accept or reject what the Bible says about homosexuality?

(?) How can the church be more effective at reaching out to and helping homosexuals?

(?) Do you think that someone who struggles with homosexual thoughts and desires can be "cured" of those desires?

For Love of the Game

Trailer

How do you connect with God?

The movie   drama/romance, PG-13

Billy Chapel (Kevin Costner) is nearing the end of his baseball career. While pitching a perfect game at Yankee Stadium, Chapel's thoughts race back and forth between his life as a professional athlete and the challenges of his love relationship with Jane (Kelly Preston).

This clip   (about 30 seconds)

▶ **Start** / 0:24:26 / Billy Chapel looks into the crowd at Yankee Stadium.

■ **Stop** / 0:25:00 / "Strike one!"

To most Yankee fans, Billy Chapel is a "has been." The major leagues don't want him any longer, and Billy knows it. He's not as young, not as fast, and not as alert as he used to be. Faced with his last year as pitcher, he knows he has to make each game count. On the field, Chapel can hear the insults from the crowd, the yelling fans, and the noise. He knows that to do well, he must "clear the mechanism." He tunes out the thousands of people around him so that he can concentrate on what is most important.

By the Book

Psalm 19:14; 46:10; 139:23-24; Matthew 26:36; Luke 5:16; 11:1-4

Where to take it

? What is solitude to you?

? How hard is it for you to get away from distractions to be with God?

? In this scene, we get a great visual image of clearing the mind of distractions and focusing. What needs to happen in your walk with God to clear "the noise" and concentrate on what he is telling you?

? In Luke 11:1-4, we are given a great model of prayer. How can you apply this to your life?

? In Matthew 26:36 and Luke 5:16, Jesus gets away to pray. Why do you think that even the son of God wanted to get away and pray?

? Why is it when the crowd seems against us, we go to God with everything, but when the crowd is cheering for us we put God on the back burner?

? Read Psalm 46:10. What do you think it means to "be still, and know that I am God?"

The Four Feathers

The movie · drama, PG-13

Harry Faversham (Heath Ledger) is a respected and dearly loved officer in a tight-knit group of soldiers. He has just announced his engagement to his beautiful love, Ethne (Kate Hudson), when news arrives of a Muslim uprising against the British in the Sudan. Harry's regiment will be sent to North Africa to fight. Suddenly and surprisingly, Harry resigns his commission. Feeling betrayed by this choice, his friends and fiancé give him white feathers, symbolizing his cowardice, and Harry's father, the General, disowns him. When the English forces arrive in Sudan, they are subject to brutal and relentless attacks. As reports begin to filter into England about what an atrocious battle it is, Harry decides to travel to Sudan to protect the very people who have branded him a coward.

This clip · (about 3 minutes)

▶ **Start** / 0:56:20 / "Are you a deserter?"

■ **Stop** / 0:59:49 / Harry waits impatiently for Abou to finish praying.

While crossing the desert of Sudan to find his friends stationed there, Harry is attacked and left for dead. Abou Fatma (Djimon Hounsou) rescues him and sees that he is nursed back to health. With Fatma's help, Harry disguises himself as a Sudanese native. He then makes his way to his friends where he can keep an eye out for their safety while they remain unaware of his presence. When some Muslim spies sneak away from the British camp, Harry and Abou follow them. The two men make camp one night, and Abou asks Harry why he is not with the British soldiers. Harry explains that he was afraid; however, Abou is not convinced. Harry has questions, too—he can't understand why an African tribesman would want to protect him. Abou tells him, "God put you in my way. I had no choice."

By the Book

2 Samuel 14:14; Luke 10:38-42; Acts 8:26-39; 1 Corinthians 16:13;
1 Thessalonians 5:14

Where to take it

? Have you ever been sent somewhere to "fight," to do something that involved risk and sacrifice, but ran away? If so, why did you run?

? Abou tells Harry, "God put you in my way. I had no choice." Describe times when God has placed certain people in your path, and you felt compelled to help. Has God put any people in your life who have helped you in your walk of faith? What did those people do for you?

? Do you believe there is such a thing as a "divine appointment," a meeting God has orchestrated, or do you believe every meeting is just coincidence, chance, or luck? What has led you to this conclusion?

? Read Acts 8:26-39. The two main people in this passage are from different nations and cultures. How did God arrange this meeting, and what was the result?

? In the last part of the movie clip, the spies are on the move. Harry is anxious to stay in close pursuit, but Abou is praying diligently. Which character best describes you: the one praying or the one impatiently rushing around?

? Read Luke 10:38-42. Discuss what you see in Mary and Martha and how they respond to Jesus' presence in their home. What does this mean to you? Is one right and one wrong? What can you learn from how Jesus handles the situation?

Groundhog Day

Trailer

Do you bring people closer to God or push them further away from him?

The movie — comedy, PG

Phil Conners (Bill Murray) is a Pittsburgh weatherman who, despite his reluctance, is sent to Punxsutawny, Pennsylvania, each year to cover the Groundhog Day celebration. After reporting the groundhog's weather forecast, Phil and his crew head out of town, only to be forced to return because of a blizzard. Phil discovers that no matter what he does, when he awakens the following morning, it is once again February 2, and he must relive his entire day—over and over again—in the town he despises.

This clip (just under 2 minutes)

▶ **Start** / 0:10:21 / Ned Ryerson stops in middle of street: "Phil?"

■ **Stop** / 0:12:07 / "Watch out for that first step. It's a doozy!"

Phil Conners is walking down Main Street in Punxsutawny on his way to the town square to find out whether the groundhog has seen its shadow. An old acquaintance from school, Ned Ryerson (Stephen Tobolowsky) recognizes Phil and starts a conversation. Clearly Ned has only one motive: to sell Phil life insurance. During this conversation, Phil realizes what a square Ned still is and wants nothing to do with him. However, the more Phil tries to get out of the conversation, the more Ned presses on, repulsing the crusty weatherman. What Phil doesn't realize is that he will have to encounter Ned Ryerson day after day until he develops some new values that change the way he interacts with people.

By the Book

Matthew 5:43-45; John 13:35; Galatians 2:20; Titus 2:11-12; 1 Peter 2:24; 4:8

Where to take it

(?) Read Matthew 5:43-45 and 1 Peter 4:8. We are commanded to love everyone. How difficult is this for you?

(?) What are some ways you can get along with people even if they annoy you?

(?) Ned Ryerson's assignment is to sell life insurance. As Christians, we are assigned to carry the good news of eternal life to others. Do you bring people closer to God or push them further away from him by your words and actions?

(?) Read Galatians 2:20, Titus 2:11-12, and 1 Peter 2:24. What do these passages say about how we, as believers, should live our lives?

(?) What do you think is the most positive trait in the way you interact with others? What would you like to change about the way you interact with others?

Hart's War

The movie drama, R

Lieutenant Tommy Hart (Colin Farrell) is a second-year law student who, due to his family's political status, is assigned a cushy clerical position far away from the fighting in World War II. One day, while on a simple chauffeur run, he gets captured, tortured for information, and then marched through brutal winter conditions to a Nazi POW camp. At the POW camp, he has a difficult time navigating the politics and prejudices of his fellow soldiers. When a black POW is accused of murdering a racist white prisoner, the top-ranking officer, Colonel William McNamara (Bruce Willis), assigns Hart to defend Lieutenant Lincoln Scott (Terrence Howard). In preparing the defense, Hart stumbles upon a plot that will force him to choose between his country, his integrity, and his life.

This clip (about 6 minutes)

▶ **Start** / 1:53:40 / "You will be the first!"

■ **Stop** / 1:59:47 / "...and so have I."

Using the trial of Lt. Scott as a cover, 35 American prisoners, led by Col. McNamara, are finishing an escape tunnel under the building. They plan to break out so they can report to Allied forces the location of active munitions factories behind the camp. German Colonel Visser (Marcel Iures) discovers the tunnel, but Col. McNamara and his men have already fled. Col. Visser orders the execution of everybody involved in the court martial and confronts Lt. Hart, telling him that he will be the first of many to be shot. Before Col. Visser can give the order, however, Col. McNamara returns to the gate of the POW camp. As the munitions factories are being bombed in the background, Col. McNamara tells Col. Visser that he is willing to take the responsibility for the escape, thus sparing the lives of the rest of the men.

By the Book

Proverbs 18:12; Matthew 20:28; John 12:46; 15:13; Romans 12:1;
Hebrews 2:9

Where to take it

(?) Col. McNamara sacrificed his life to save the others. Do you think he was brave or foolish? Would you do this for your friends? Would you do this for total strangers?

(?) How would you feel if someone gave up his life to save yours?

(?) Share a story about sacrifice that involves you or someone you know. How has it impacted your life?

(?) Read Matthew 20:28 and John 12:46. According to these passages, what did Jesus come to do? Why do you think so many people reject Jesus and what he did?

(?) Read Romans 12:1. What kind of sacrifice does this verse refer to? How do you think this kind of surrender works on a daily basis?

(?) Col. McNamara knew that, as a leader, he was responsible for the welfare of his men. Are there people you are responsible for? What do you give up for their sake?

Hometown Legend

Trailer

There are times when coming together as a team means everything.

The movie — drama/religion, PG

Athens High School was legendary in the world of Alabama football. When the school's hard-driving Coach Schuler (Terry O'Quinn) loses his son in an on-field collision during a game, he leaves the team and the town. In the 12 years that follow, Athens High School dwindles and is about to be shut down. The only thing drawing students to the school is a scholarship for college offered to one player each year in honor and memory of Coach Schuler's son. In its final season, Coach Schuler returns to coach the Crusader team for the last time. Elvis Jackson (Nick Cornish), a drifter who has ideas of making the team and earning his own ticket to college, also arrives in town that season.

This clip (about 4 minutes)

▶ **Start** / 1:23:23 / "All right God, you got something to say to me?"

■ **Stop** / 1:28:04 / "That's something I've never had before."

Since coming to Athens, Elvis has worked hard to win the acceptance of his demanding coach as well as qualify for the scholarship. Bouncing between foster homes for most of his life, Elvis learned to look out for his own interests; however, having a part in revitalizing the football team and the town of Athens and meeting Rachel (Lacey Chabert) begins to change what Elvis believes. When Elvis gets hurt right before the championship game and subsequently finds out there is no money to fund the scholarship, he decides to give up and leave. Rachel challenges him to look at who and what he is really playing for, encouraging him to see the bigger picture and plan for his life.

By the Book

Isaiah 55:8; Romans 8:31; 12:5; Ephesians 3:20; 1 Timothy 4:12

Where to take it

? Describe a time in your life when you knew that "God was the only explanation" for something that happened.

? How does God speak to you? Do you ever quiet yourself so you can hear God's "still small voice"?

? How can the body of Christ make a difference in your community, school, or church youth group?

? Describe a time when you were part of a team or community that joined together and accomplished something incredible.

? What are some benefits of being part of a team?

? Does God use others to teach you about himself? About life? Who, in your life, has God used this way?

Trailer

Do you swear to tell the truth,
so help you God?

The movie — drama, PG-13

Sam Dawson (Sean Penn) is a mentally challenged man who lives in a small apartment in Los Angeles. He has a group of devoted friends, a job at the local Starbucks, and a young daughter named Lucy (Dakota Fanning), whom he's been raising by himself. When Lucy is seven years old, she begins to surpass her father's mental capacity and starts to hold herself back at school because she doesn't want to "outgrow" her father. When the authorities discover this and take Lucy to foster care, Sam must find a way to keep his daughter in his life.

This clip (just under 2 minutes)

▶ **Start** / 1:08:47 / "Raise your right hand."

■ **Stop** / 1:11:07 / "All you need is love."

As part of the court hearing, Lucy is placed under oath in order to be questioned about her father. A live video feed is connected to the courtroom for Sam to see. When Lucy lies to the prosecution in an attempt to save her father's dignity, Sam is saddened and encourages the TV image of his daughter to tell the truth.

By the Book

Psalm 51:6; 120:2; Proverbs 14:5; 21:28; Ephesians 4:25; Colossians 3:9-10

Where to take it

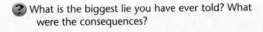

? What is the biggest lie you have ever told? What were the consequences?

? Do you remember when you told your first lie? What did you lie about?

? List all the reasons you can think of for not telling the truth. In what situations do you find it most difficult to be honest?

? What is the most destructive thing about lying? Describe a time when you were hurt because of your own or someone else's lies.

? Sir Walter Scott wrote, "Oh what a tangled web we weave when first we practice to deceive." Do you believe this quote? Can you describe any examples of deception leading to a tangled web in your life?

? What do Ephesians 4:25 and Colossians 3:9-10 say about lying and telling the truth?

? In the clip, Lucy states that all she needs is love. What is the one basic thing you need from your parents? What about from your friends?

What does your "herd" look like?

The movie · family/animation, PG

With an ice age approaching, prehistoric animals are migrating south to new lands and warmer climates. When Manfred the Mammoth (voiced by Ray Romano) decides to "pass" on the migration, he meets Sid the Sloth (voiced by John Leguizamo), whose relatives didn't bother to wake him when they left. Manfred is not too keen on his new friend, but when the two come across a baby who has been lost, he agrees with Sid that they should return the baby to its tribe. Along the way, they run into a Saber-toothed tiger named Diego (voiced by Denis Leary), who also desires to help. What Manfred and Sid don't know is that Diego has an ulterior motive. His fellow tigers have chosen him to lead Manfred, Sid, and the baby into an ambush. As the group makes its way across the icy wilderness, they find that even an unlikely group of friends can learn to watch out for one another.

This clip (about 2 minutes)

▶ **Start** / 0:53:13 / "My feet are sweaty."

■ **Stop** / 0:55:55 / "I don't know about you guys, but we are the weirdest herd I've ever seen."

Everything is on the line as the three reluctant friends find themselves in the middle of a lava flow. While running to safety, Manfred rescues Diego from falling into the molten pit and almost gets himself killed. Once they are clear of the danger, Diego asks why Manfred would risk his life for him. Manfred tells him, "That's what you do in a herd—you look out for each other." Diego, thinking about his own plans to trap Manfred and make a meal out of him, is amazed at the thought of that kind of sacrifice.

By the Book

Proverbs 17:17; 18:24; 27:5-6; Ecclesiastes 4:9-12; John 15:13;
1 Corinthians 10:24; 1 Thessalonians 5:11

Where to take it

? In detail, describe your "herd" (your friends). Explain what you like about them and why they are important to you.

? Does your herd have the same kind of people in it, or is it a mix of different types, more like the group in the movie? Do you think differences make a group stronger or weaker? Are there are any traits you need to have in common to be a good herd? If so, then what are they?

? What do you think makes you a good friend? What qualities do you look for in a friend?

? Diego asks Manfred, "You could have died trying to save me. Why did you do that?" Manfred replies, "That's what you do in a herd. You look out for each other." How do you look out for your friends? How do they look out for you? What would you do and how far would you go for a friend?

? John 15:13 says that a person can have no greater love than to lay down his or her life for a friend. What does this mean to you?

? Describe a time when you faced a hardship and your friends pulled you through.

Insomnia

Trailer

What are you trying to escape from?

The movie thriller, R

Los Angeles detective Will Dormer (Al Pacino) cannot sleep. Internal Affairs is investigating him for corruption, and he discovers that his partner, Hap Eckhart (Martin Donovan), plans to cut a deal with Internal Affairs. To avoid public scrutiny, the two cops are sent to Nightmute, Alaska, to investigate the murder of a 17-year-old girl. They set a trap for the suspected killer, Walter Finch (Robin Williams). However, in the fog, Dormer accidentally shoots and kills Eckhart. Finch sees the shooting and contacts Dormer to make an offer—he will keep quiet about what he witnessed if Dormer will pin this crime on someone else. Unable to escape the Alaskan midnight sun or his conscience, Will Dormer spends night after sleepless night wrestling with the choices he has made.

This clip (just under 2 1/2 minutes)

▶ **Start** / 1:40:00 / "The second I met this guy, Dobbs...I knew he was guilty."

◼ **Stop** / 1:42:22 / "I guess it's what you thought was right at the time and what you are willing to live with."

Sleep deprivation is diminishing Will's ability to reason, and no matter how hard he tries, he cannot get his room dark enough to get any rest. When the woman who works at the hotel (Maura Tierney) comes to his room to check on him, Will tells her about his secret and his guilt. He wonders whether the ends ever justify the means and reveals the events that led to his decision to walk down the wrong path. Now the consequences of his decisions threaten his future, and he has to decide what he can live with: being "not guilty" in the eyes of others or innocent in his own soul.

By the Book

Ezra 9:6; Psalm 32:5; 38:4; Isaiah 43:18; 44:22; Matthew 11:28; Colossians 3:25

Where to take it

(?) Have you ever done something that is wrong for what you thought were all the right reasons?

(?) Will states, "I could feel it right then. This is going to catch up with me." Have you ever done something you knew wasn't right, but you did it anyway? Have the consequences caught up with you?

(?) Does the end always justify the means? Explain why you agree or disagree.

(?) In your daily life, what do you find yourself avoiding? People, situations, pain?

(?) Will can't sleep because guilt over his actions is eating him up inside. How does your guilt express itself?

(?) Do you find yourself living in your past or going over and over previous decisions and actions?

(?) Is there a part of your past that is difficult to live with or is a burden? What part of your past are you ready to give over to God?

Trailer

What if we lived in a world
with no parents?

The movie   animation, G

Little Jimmy Neutron (voiced by Debi Derryberry) is only a kid, but he has the mind of a genius. Jimmy gets teased by his classmates, and his inventions are misunderstood. What frustrates Jimmy even more is that his parents cannot comprehend his amazing talents and skills. When aliens kidnap all the adults in the city, it's up to Jimmy Neutron to lead his classmates to find out just what went down in his hometown.

This clip   (just under 6 minutes)

▶ **Start** / 0:33:29 / "Wouldn't it be great if our folks all disappeared for awhile?"

⬛ **Stop** / 0:39:26 / "What kind of parents take off and leave their kid?"

One morning, Jimmy awakens to find a note from his parents explaining that they have left town to go to Florida for an extended vacation. When he goes around his neighborhood, he finds that all the other kids' parents are gone as well. Chaos breaks out as the youngsters take over the town. With no parents to tell them what to do, they eat whatever they want, wear whatever they want, stay up late, and throw a big party. The day after, however, is not as much fun as the first day, not only because the children experience the consequences of their excesses, but also because they feel the void that is left by their parents' absence.

By the Book

Psalm 103:13; Proverbs 19:27; 22:6; 29:15; Galatians 5:13; Ephesians 6:1

Where to take it

? When you were younger, did you ever wish your parents would disappear? Do you ever still wish they would disappear?

? What do you like about your parents? What do you wish was different about your parents?

? Do you know someone whose parents are absent because of divorce, death, or another circumstance?

? Does comparing your life to that person's make you thankful for your family?

? In this clip, all the kids in the city go crazy doing and eating anything they want. The next day is a little different. Describe a time when you were given the freedom to do whatever you wanted and regretted your decisions later.

? Read Psalm 103:13 and Proverbs 22:6. What do these verses say about the role parents have in our lives?

? Read Proverbs 29:15 and Ephesians 6:1. What do these verses say about how children should act toward and react to their parents? Is this hard to do when your parents are not following Scripture?

What are you afraid of?

The movie   comedy, PG

Joe Scheffer (Tim Allen) is starting to believe he is a nobody. He wife has left him for another man, he works in a small cubicle making video spots for a large pharmaceutical company, and for the last 10 years he has been passed over for promotions and ignored by most of the other employees. The only person who seems to think that Joe is somebody is his 12-year-old daughter, Natalie (Hayden Panettiere). One morning, Joe gets into a dispute over a parking space, and Mark McKinney (Patrick Warburton) hits him in front of his daughter and his coworkers. Feeling something was taken from him that he must get back, Joe challenges the bully to a rematch. This bold move wins him the admiration of his fellow employees who can't stand McKinney, either. It could, however, cost him his daughter's respect and his new girlfriend's (Julie Bowen) love. Joe must decide who he is and who he is not willing to be.

This clip   (just under 3 minutes)

▶ **Start** / 0:11:37 / "Wait a minute, wait a minute! Are you threatening to hit me?"

⏹ **Stop** / 0:15:05 / "Disappearing, I think."

Joe doesn't realize that his life is about to change when he and Natalie enter the parking lot on "Bring Your Daughter to Work Day." As he looks for a parking space in the "10-year associate lot," Joe gets cut off by the company bully, Mark McKinney, who has been with the firm for only seven years. When Joe insists that Mark find a new spot, Mark smacks him around and humiliates him in front of his coworkers and his daughter. Paralyzed by embarrassment, Joe hides in his house in an attempt to escape his life. Natalie calls to check on him and finds that he is lost in excuses and fear.

By the Book

Psalm 91:14-15; Isaiah 54:4; Matthew 18:1-4; Luke 9:12-17; John 13:12-17; Romans 12:17-18; Hebrews 13:6

Where to take it

? Have you ever seen someone close to you get hurt? How did it affect you?

? Have any "heroes" in your life fallen off of their pedestals? How did it happen?

? When her dad avoids her, Natalie asks, "Is it you don't want to see me, or is it you don't want me to see you?" Have you ever avoided someone because you were embarrassed?

? How much do you value others' image of you? How do you protect your image?

? Right now, what scares you?

? Natalie asks her dad what he is afraid of, and he replies that he is scared of disappearing. What does his answer mean to you? Can you relate to this fear?

? Read Matthew 18:1-4, Luke 9:46-48, and John 13:12-17. In these passages, what does Christ say about the qualities of greatness in a person? How is Christ's definition of being "a somebody" in his kingdom different from the world's definition of greatness?

Trailer

Nothing is deeper than a father's love for his son.

The movie drama, PG-13

When their son, Mikey (Daniel E. Smith), collapses during a baseball game, John (Denzel Washington) and his wife, Denise (Kimberly Elise), race him to the hospital. They discover that he has a serious heart condition with very little time to live, and the only thing that will save him is a transplant that John's insurance will not pay for. The hospital gives them two options: pay cash for the $250,000 procedure or wait for their son to die. Even after selling everything they own and searching everywhere for help, they cannot raise the money. Enraged by the news that the hospital is going to send his critically ill son home, John Q becomes desperate, taking the cardiologist and the people in the emergency room hostage until Mikey is put on the organ recipient list. With the media, the police, and SWAT teams outside the hospital doors, John Q realizes that he has put himself in an impossible situation and that the only way for his son to get a transplant is to give him his own heart.

This clip (just under 5 minutes)

▶ **Start** / 1:33:01 / "This is my will. Says I'm leaving my heart to my son."

■ **Stop** / 1:38:25 / "I love you, son."

With his back against the wall and time running out, John Q will not let his son die. He decides to give Mikey his heart in order to save his life. John goes to his son's bedside to say goodbye. Knowing that he will not be there to guide him as he grows up, John tells Mikey the values and attributes that he wants him to have throughout his life.

By the Book

Psalm 139; John 3:16; 15:13; Romans 5:8; 2 Timothy 2:22; 1 John 3:1; 4:10

Where to take it

? Would you give your life so that someone else could live?

? Watch the section of the clip in which John lists a number of different values he wants his son to hold on to. Which of the values on this list are important to you? Why? Which values would you take off the list? Why?

? If God could have a talk with you like the talk John Q has with Mikey, what values do you think he would want you to have in your life?

? This father is going to give up his life so his son can live. Read John 3:16. What kind of sacrifice is this verse describing?

? Read Psalm 139. What does it say about how God thinks about each one of us?

? Read Romans 5:8, 1 John 3:1, and 1 John 4:10. What do these verses say about how much God loves us?

Kate and Leopold

Trailer

Where have all the manners gone?

The movie — comedy, PG-13

Love seems to come and go for Kate (Meg Ryan), a single businesswoman trying to work her way to the top. Her progress in her career is, at times, thwarted by chauvinistic men in the industry. Discovering a rip in the fabric of time, Kate's ex-boyfriend, Stuart (Liev Schreiber), travels back to the late 1800s and finds Leopold (Hugh Jackman), the third Duke of Albany, who is under pressure to marry but can't find a woman who thinks for herself. Noticing Stuart because he is out of place, Leopold follows him back through the portal to the 21st century. As Kate and Leopold get acquainted, they find each other a refreshing, if odd, change from the people they usually meet.

This clip [about 3 minutes]

▶ **Start** / 0:36:44 / "I invited someone to dinner."

⏹ **Stop** / 0:40:00 / "Goodnight, Leo."

Kate's brother, Charlie (Breckin Meyer), invites Leopold for dinner. Throughout the meal, Kate and Charlie are surprised by Leopold's kind manners, and he tries to explain why he believes it is important to show a lady respect. Kate is taken aback by the way this man, who claims to be from the 19th century, treats her and is actually uncomfortable around Leopold because she isn't used to the respect and honor he shows her. The men she usually dates are not so well mannered. Despite her discomfort, though, perhaps she does want to be swept off her feet by a courteous gentleman.

By the Book

Proverbs 15:1; Luke 6:31; 1 Corinthians 13:4-7; 2 Timothy 2:24; Titus 3:1-2; 1 Peter 3:4

Where to take it

(?) What do you think is the purpose of good manners?

(?) Do you think the world we live in has forgotten what it means to show respect and kindness to people? Why do you think this is so?

(?) Describe a rude person. How do you react to someone like this? What is the most inconsiderate thing you have ever done to someone?

(?) Does your family still sit down for dinner—or any meal—to talk about the day? Why or why not?

(?) When Kate gets up from the table, Leo stands because it is courteous. What are some other "courtesies" we seldom observe any more?

(?) How do Luke 6:31 and 2 Timothy 2:24 instruct us to treat people? Which of these instructions do you need to work on most?

(?) Do you think that being a "gentleman" or a "nice young lady" is dull?

Trailer
What "laws" keep our world
from crumbling?

The movie — drama, PG-13

Dr. Mark Powell (Jeff Bridges) meets his new patient, Prot (Kevin Spacey), who has been placed in the psychiatric facility for claiming to be a visitor from the planet K-PAX. Dr. Powell thinks that Prot is suffering from delusions. It is not long, however, before Prot's knowledge and behavior begin to alter not only the doctor's diagnosis but also the mental conditions of his fellow patients, and each encounter with Prot leads Dr. Powell to question himself more than his patient. Because Prot's stories are so complete and intriguing, Dr. Powell is determined to find out the truth. What he may discover is that the impossible can become possible, even in his own life.

This clip — (about 3 minutes)

▶ **Start** / 0:23:45 / "Good morning, Joyce. That's a lovely configuration you are wearing today."

■ **Stop** / 0:26:47 / "Sometimes it's hard to imagine how you've made it this far."

Trying to discover who Prot really is and what has made him want to escape reality, Dr. Powell asks him about his family. Prot says that on K-PAX there are no such things as marriage or families. Prot paints a picture of K-PAX that is extremely different from Earth: the whole community raises the children, and there is no need for government or laws. Unable to understand this, Dr. Powell asks what happens when someone does something wrong. Prot tells Powell that all beings know right from wrong. He believes the problem on Earth might be that humans do not follow what they know to be true.

By the Book

Exodus 20:1-17; Deuteronomy 7:9; Proverbs 8:15;
Matthew 5:38-42; 22:34-40; Romans 13:1-3; Titus 3:1

Where to take it

? Would you want the type of life that Prot says exists on K-PAX?

? What makes our planet unique? What do you appreciate about where you live?

? Prot tells Dr. Powell that every being in the universe knows right from wrong. Explain why you agree or disagree with this.

? Do you believe in an "eye for an eye" and a life for a life?

? Prot says that Christians haven't paid attention to Christ's words and teachings. In general, how true do you think this statement is? Do you believe you listen to God and focus your life on the truth of his Word? How do you do this?

? Read the Ten Commandments in Exodus 20:1-17. How are the laws of our country similar to God's laws? How are they different?

? Read Matthew 22:34-40, in which Jesus lays out the two greatest commandments. Now, go back and look at the original Ten Commandments given to Moses. How does the shortened version (that Jesus teaches) incorporate the original version?

The Last Castle

The movie   drama, R

General Irwin (Robert Redford) is a military legend. However, he makes a mistake, and eight of his men lose their lives. Court-martialed and stripped of his rank, the former three-star general has been sentenced to the maximum-security military prison run by a power-hungry and rigidly strict warden, Colonel Winter (James Gandolfini). Irwin is content to serve his sentence quietly and in peace until he becomes aware that Col. Winter is running a brutally violent operation inside the castle walls. With the help of his fellow inmates, Irwin orchestrates an uprising in the prison. This leads to a climactic showdown between the two kings of the military castle.

This clip   (about 3 minutes)

▶ **Start** / 0:24:50 / "You're late. You have five minutes left on your visitor."

■ **Stop** / 0:28:04 / "When I was in first grade, I got straight As."

Irwin's daughter (Robin Wright Penn) visits him inside the castle. The two soon realize that their relationship has been so distant for so many years they have nothing to say to one another. Although his daughter tries to come up with small talk, she quickly becomes frustrated because the things she thought she always wanted to say don't seem to matter anymore. Irwin wants to get to know her, and he tries to give her some hope that they can develop a relationship now.

By the Book

Psalm 103:13; Malachi 4:6; 2 Corinthians 6:18; Ephesians 4:31; Colossians 3:21

Where to take it

? Irwin's estranged daughter makes a visit and finds that she really has nothing to say. How does your relationship with your father compare to the one in the clip?

? Irwin's daughter tells her dad that she had a whole list of things to say to him, but now, none of them seems to matter. Have you ever had a list of things you wanted to talk with your dad about? Whether positive or negative, what was on it?

? Have you ever told your dad how you feel about your relationship? If you did, what would you say to him?

? What does a child need from a father?

? In general, how would you describe the relationship most teens have with their fathers today? How much time would you say most fathers spend with their children? What effects do today's typical father-child relationships seem to have on this generation of teens?

? What values do you hope to teach your children?

Trailer

Passion could be the key ingredient to abundant living.

The movie comedy, PG-13

Elle Woods (Reese Witherspoon) is president of her sorority and easily gets a 4.0 grade point average in her major—fashion design. She is thrilled that her Harvard-bound boyfriend, Warner (Matthew Davis), is about to propose to her. When he dumps her because she doesn't fit the image of a politician's wife, Elle sets her sights on getting into Harvard to win him back. What Elle doesn't realize is that the classes at Harvard Law School are not the most difficult part of her quest. She must battle the prejudices of her professors, fellow students, and Warner's new fiancée to prove that she is more than what she appears.

This clip (about 3 minutes)

▶ **Start** / 1:28:29 / "Ladies and gentlemen, the graduates of Harvard Law School."

■ **Stop** / 1:31:50 / Graduation scene fades.

Elle delivers a graduation speech to her peers at Harvard Law School. In her speech, she disagrees with the Greek philosopher Aristotle, who said that the law is reason free from passion. Elle says that with no disrespect to Aristotle, she has come to find that passion is a key ingredient to the study and practice of law. Elle goes on to say that passion is necessary for life.

By the Book

Genesis 6:13-27; Esther 2:7-8:7; Daniel 3:12-30; John 6:39-40; 17:25-26;
2 Corinthians 5:15; 8:7; Philippians 1:21

Where to take it

? This clip shows what happens to different people after graduation. What do you desire to have predicted about your future?

? What does the word *passion* mean to you? What are you passionate about?

? Do you think many people lead passionless lives? Why or why not?

? Elle presents several values of a passionate life. Which values do you agree with? Which do you disagree with? What others would you add?

? Elle mentions conviction as an important value. How would you define conviction? How much of a driving force are convictions in your life? Name your top convictions.

? Read John 6:39-40 and John 17:25-26. What was Jesus' greatest passion? How different are your desires from his?

? Look up some of these men and women of the Bible: Noah in Genesis 6:13-22; Shadrach, Meshach, and Abednego in Daniel 3:12-30; and Esther in Esther 2:7-8:7. These people had passion, faith, and conviction. How do these people's stories affect you?

The Legend of Bagger Vance

Trailer
Lay your burdens down.

The movie   drama, PG-13

Rannulph Junuh (Matt Damon) was the golden boy of Savannah, Georgia, because of the way he played golf. When the U.S. enters World War I, Junuh enlists and returns home a battered, tortured soul. Becoming a recluse, drowning his sorrows in liquor, and trying not to think about what his life has become, he loses the respect of the town, the affections of his girlfriend, and his golf swing. As the Depression takes its toll on Savannah, his former love, Adele (Charlize Theron) takes matters into her own hands and organizes a golf tournament for the biggest names in the game. Savannah's town leaders approve of the idea on one condition: a local golfer must be allowed to play in the match. An inspirational caddie named Bagger Vance (Will Smith) appears on the scene one night while Junuh is trying to prepare for the competition. With Bagger's wisdom and guidance, Junuh sets out to rediscover his swing—and his soul.

This clip   (about 4 minutes)

▶ **Start** / 1:38:34 / Junuh walking through trees to find his golf ball

⏹ **Stop** / 1:42:36 / Junuh hearing cheers after he lands the golf ball on the green

Junuh has a rough start in the tournament but begins to turn his game around when he, once again, feels the desire to win. At a pivotal point in the game, he hits a shot into the woods. When he steps through the trees to find his ball, scenes from the war flash through his mind and create havoc with his emotions. Nearly immobilized by fear, Junuh bends down to pick up his ball, thereby disqualifying himself from playing the hole. Bagger Vance intervenes and encourages Junuh to lay down the burdens of his past and get back in the game.

By the Book

Psalm 30:4-5; 55:22; Isaiah 43:18; Matthew 11:28-29; John 16:33;
Ephesians 1:3-6; 2 Thessalonians 2:13-14

Where to take it

(?) While walking through the trees, Junuh's memories of the war return, paralyzing him. His past haunts him. What in your past stops you "dead in your tracks"?

(?) Why is "I can't do this" such a powerful statement?

(?) Bagger Vance says everyone carries some burden that he doesn't understand. Describe what a "burden" is. What are your burdens? Why do you think God allows us to bear burdens that we do not understand?

(?) Read Psalm 55:22 and Matthew 11:28-30. What do these passages say about burdens?

(?) Bagger tells Junuh that it is time for him to come out of the shadows and choose to start playing the game again. In what way does this advice apply to you?

(?) Consider this statement from the clip: "Play the game...your game... the one that only you can play...the one that was given to you when you came into this world." How does this relate to how you should live your life? How does Bagger's encouragement to Junuh compare to Ephesians 1:3-6 and 2 Thessalonians 2:13-14?

Life or Something Like it

Trailer

Are there modern-day "prophets" walking among us?

The movie   comedy, PG-13

Lanie Kerrigan (Angelina Jolie) is a feature reporter at a Seattle news station. She carefully constructs every moment of her life to project the right image. She has a great apartment, the right hair, and physical beauty; she's also engaged to the star player of Seattle's baseball team. By her own admission, nothing can bother her because her life is perfect. And she is not bothered until she interviews a homeless man who claims to be a prophet. In one conversation, Prophet Jack (Tony Shalhoub) gives three predictions. Lanie walks away rattled because one of his prophecies is that she will die within a week. After Prophet Jack's first two predictions come true, Lanie begins to look within herself, and, in light of her approaching death, discovers the shallowness and purposelessness of her "perfect" life.

This clip   (just under 4 minutes)

▶ **Start** / 0:12:10 / Prophet Jack pushes his "pedestal" into the middle of downtown Seattle.

■ **Stop** / 0:16:37 / "Tonight Seahawks over the Broncos...take the points."

Lanie's cameraman (Ed Burns) sets up an interview between Lanie and Prophet Jack. She doesn't take the meeting very seriously and asks Prophet Jack more questions about the fate of Seattle's football team than about him and his prophetic giftedness. Lanie is in full control of the conversation, even poking fun at Prophet Jack...until he reveals that she will die before the week is over.

By the Book

Deuteronomy 18:20; James 4:13-15; 2 Peter 1:20-21; 1 John 4:1

Where to take it

- What is a prophet? Do you think there are any modern-day prophets?

- Do you think prophets hear God differently from the way other people hear God? Do you hear the voice of God? How do you know that it's God's voice?

- Think about the prophets in the Bible. How do they differ from what you think a modern-day prophet would be like? Do you think that a modern-day prophet would be treated the same way as one from biblical times?

- Define *prophecy*. What do you think is the purpose of prophecy?

- What if you were told you had one week to live? Would you live your life differently? What would you start doing? What would you stop doing?

- How do you measure the significance and purpose of your life?

The Lord of The Rings: The Fellowship of the Rings

Trailer

Do you like adventure or comfort?

The movie   sci-fi/drama, PG-13

Bilbo Baggins (Ian Holm) gives his young cousin, Frodo (Elijah Wood), a ring that he found on one of his many adventures. Dark Lord Sauron forged the ring, and it has only one purpose: to command Sauron's own army to conquer and enslave all of Middle Earth. Also, the ring has the power to corrupt anyone who holds it. Because he believes in the purity of Frodo's heart, Bilbo feels that the ring will be safe in his cousin's keeping. After Bilbo gives the ring to Frodo, Frodo finds he must travel into the heart of Mordor to cast the ring into the fires of Mount Doom. He sets off with his friends to make the perilous journey to destroy the ring before it falls into the wrong hands.

This clip   (about 1 minute)

▶ **Start** / 0:37:16 / Frodo and Sam walk along the countryside.

■ **Stop** / 0:38:20 / "There's no knowing where you might be swept off to."

Frodo and his friend, Sam (Sean Astin), set out on an adventure that will take them into a world that is unknown to them. At one point, Sam stops as Frodo walks on. When Frodo asks what he is doing, Sam explains that he is standing at the farthest place he has ever gone without turning around and going back home. One more step, and he is in uncharted territory. With Frodo's encouragement, Sam takes the step that will change both of their lives forever.

By the Book

Deuteronomy 31:6; 2 Chronicles 15:7; Psalm 23:4; Proverbs 27:17; Romans 8:35-37; Ephesians 6:16; Hebrews 11:6; James 1:2-3

Where to take it

- Sam says to Frodo, "If I take one more step, it's the farthest away from home I've ever been." Describe a time when you have felt like this. Did you continue or did you turn back?

- Why do you think people are afraid to take risks?

- Read Proverbs 27:17. Do you think Frodo was sharpening Sam? Do you have friends who keep you accountable and encourage you to go farther in your walk with God?

- Sam takes the step. In your life, where is God calling you to take a step of faith?

- In the clip, Bilbo says, "It's a dangerous business going out your front door." How is this true? What are the benefits and risks of courageous faith? What kind of courage do you think you possess?

- Read Psalm 23:4, Romans 8:35-37, and James 1:2-3. What kinds of images for stepping out in faith do these passages give?

- Ralph Waldo Emerson writes, "Do the thing we fear, and the death of fear is certain." What does this mean to you in your journey?

The Lord of The Rings: The Fellowship of the Rings

What has a hold on your life?

The movie / sci-fi/drama, PG-13

Bilbo Baggins (Ian Holm) gives his young cousin, Frodo (Elijah Wood), a ring that he found on one of his many adventures. Dark Lord Sauron forged the ring, and it has only one purpose: to command Sauron's own army to conquer and enslave all of Middle Earth. Also, the ring has the power to corrupt anyone who holds it. Because he believes in the purity of Frodo's heart, Bilbo feels that the ring will be safe in his cousin's keeping. After Bilbo gives the ring to Frodo, Frodo finds he must travel into the heart of Mordor to cast the ring into the fires of Mount Doom. He sets off with his friends to make the perilous journey to destroy the ring before it falls into the wrong hands.

This clip (about 1 minute)

▶ **Start** / 1:33:34 / "My old sword...here take it."

■ **Stop** / 1:35:14 / Bilbo grabs Frodo's hand.

Bilbo Baggins and Frodo meet once again on Frodo's journey to Mount Doom. The older Hobbit attempts to prepare young Frodo for battle by giving him a sword and a mesh suit for protection. While encouraging Frodo to try on the suit, Bilbo notices the ring on a chain around Frodo's neck, and he asks to hold the ring just one more time. Seeing the power the ring has over Bilbo, Frodo does not allow him to touch it. Bilbo's demeanor turns almost demonic as he lunges at Frodo to snatch the ring from him.

By the Book

Matthew 26:41; John 10:10; Romans 7:15-20; 8:26; 1 Corinthians 10:13; Galatians 5:16-17; 1 Peter 5:8-9

Where to take it

(?) Bilbo almost crumbles under his desire for the ring, which is his weakness. Even in the midst of your strengths, what is your biggest weakness (your ring)?

(?) Read 1 Peter 5:8-9. What does this passage mean to your walk with God?

(?) In the presence of the ring and with a chance to touch it, Bilbo changes before Frodo's eyes. How does your character change when you want something that isn't good for you?

(?) Can you describe a time when you wanted something that only brought you pain?

(?) What do you think is inside us that makes us want what isn't good for us?

(?) Have you ever given up something, only to have it come into your life again? Tell your story.

(?) Read Matthew 26:41, 1 Corinthians 10:13, and Galatians 5:16-17. What do these verses say about how to avoid evil and the things that bring us down?

Trailer
What defines you?

The movie **romantic comedy, PG-13**

Marisa Ventura (Jennifer Lopez) is a single mom who works as a maid in an upscale New York hotel. While tending to the cleaning duties in the Park Suite, one of her coworkers convinces Marisa to try on the designer clothes of a hotel guest. When Senate candidate Christopher Marshall (Ralph Fiennes) sees her, he mistakenly assumes that she is a hotel guest. Marisa doesn't discourage him from believing this. Chris asks Marisa to a benefit dinner, and she decides to go, but she plans to break it off when the evening is over. Unfortunately, she can't seem to cut the ties she's forming with Chris, and, when her secret is revealed, their relationship is put to the test.

This clip **(just under 5 minutes)**

▶ **Start** / 1:21:42 / "This would never have happened at the Four Seasons."

■ **Stop** / 1:26:30 / Marisa walks away after confession to Chris; Chris stands, taking it in.

The real occupant of the Park Suite, Caroline (Natasha Richardson), attends the benefit dinner and recognizes Marisa as the hotel maid. The next morning, Caroline goes to the hotel management and accuses Marisa of stealing. After being confronted by her employers, Marisa is fired. However, Marisa's supervisor, Lionel (Bob Hoskins), doesn't approve of her treatment and quits. When Chris discovers that the woman he has been pursuing isn't who he thought she was, he confronts Marisa. Marisa asks him to consider whether he would have ever looked at her if he had met her as a maid.

By the Book

Proverbs 16:19; Matthew 6:19-21; 16:26; Mark 9:35; Luke 22:26; John 12:26

Where to take it

? Lionel tells Marisa that sometimes we are forced into directions we ought to have found for ourselves. Have you ever been forced into a situation or into making a decision that you should have chosen yourself?

? What are ways that you enjoy serving others? What are some areas where you feel you need to become more of a servant?

? What do Mark 9:35 and Luke 22:26 say about becoming a true servant?

? Lionel says, "What we do does not define who we are...What defines us is how well we rise after falling." How well do you rise after falling? What gets you past the failures in your life? Can you tell about a time when your faith has grown or your character has changed after "falling"?

? What does *significance* mean to you? What defines the worth and the meaning of your life?

? On a scale of 1 to 10 (10 being the greatest), where are you on the "true joy" scale? How is it possible to find joy apart from a job, another person, friends, clothes, or money?

? Read Matthew 16:26. Are you trying to gain anything that might cause you to lose focus of who you were created to be?

How do you pray?

The movie   comedy, PG-13

Greg Focker (Ben Stiller) plans to marry his girlfriend, Pam (Teri Polo). He has picked out a beautiful ring and planned the perfect way to propose. Just before Greg pops the question, however, he finds out that Pam's father is the kind of dad who wants to be asked for his daughter's hand in marriage. Greg postpones his plans until he can obtain Pam's father's blessing. During a weekend visit to Pam's family home in New York, Greg gets his chance. Pam's father, Jack (Robert De Niro), is an intimidating ex-CIA agent who is suspicious of Greg from the start. While Greg does everything he can to be the perfect guest and future son-in-law, everything that can go wrong does go wrong. The harder Greg tries to make a good impression, the worse his situation gets.

This clip   (about 2 minutes)

▶ **Start** / 0:24:00 / Exterior of Byrnes' house.

■ **Stop** / 0:26:14 / "Thank you Greg. That was interesting, too."

The Byrnes family and Greg sit down to eat a meal together. All seems to go well until Mrs. Byrnes asks Greg to say the blessing over the meal. It is clear that Greg has no idea what to say. As he twists and turns, Greg utters an elaborate collection of sayings in order to make his prayer sound legitimate. However, no one in the family is fooled—this guy hasn't prayed a day in his life.

110

By the Book

Matthew 6:5-6, 9-13; Ephesians 6:18; Philippians 4:6; 1 Thessalonians 5:16-18

Where to take it

? In this scene, Greg is uncomfortable praying. Are you comfortable praying in a group setting? What about praying alone?

? Why do you think Greg is uncomfortable praying?

? What does prayer mean to you?

? Greg prays a prayer from St. Francis Assisi:
   Day by day, three things we pray:
   To see thee more clearly,
   To love thee more dearly,
   To follow thee more nearly,
   Day by day.
What do you pray for every day?

? What does it mean to be religious? What does it mean to have a "relationship" with God? What are the differences between the two?

? What does Scripture say about prayer in Matthew 6:5-6 and Philippians 4:16?

? Matthew 6:9-13 shows us how Jesus prayed. What can you learn from his example of prayer and what it meant to him?

Men of Honor

Trailer

When being the best isn't
good enough.

The movie   drama, R

In the 1950s, African-Americans had only two possibilities in the Navy: a cook or an officer's assistant. Although Carl Brashear (Cuba Gooding, Jr.) left school after the seventh grade and was the son of a poor sharecropper, he was determined that his destiny would be different. Before stepping on the bus to enlist in the Navy, Carl's father encourages him: "When it gets hard—and it will get hard—promise me that you will not quit." Carl keeps that pledge to his father even though he has to overcome racial intolerance and a crippling injury, as well as the hard-driving and unfair tactics of Master Chief Billy Sunday (Robert De Niro) to make his dream a reality. Most people would give up and accept defeat, but Carl perseveres to become the Navy's first African-American master diver.

This clip   (about 11 minutes)

▶ **Start** / 1:08:10 / Chief Sunday looks at picture of Carl's father.

◼ **Stop** / 1:19:17 / "Get him inside."

The night before the final diving test, Master Chief Sunday is called into the office of Base Commander Pappy (Hal Holbrook). There, Pappy gives Sunday orders that Carl is not to be allowed to pass under any circumstances. Sunday tells Carl that attempting the test is pointless because the powers that be don't want him to be a diver. Carl ignores Sunday's warnings and arrives for the chance to prove himself as a master diver by completing a drill in the cold winter waters. The Commander gives the signal for Sunday to dump the tools required for assembling the test apparatus into the murky waters so that Carl has no chance of finding them and would have to concede.

By the Book

Jeremiah 29:11; Luke 1:37; 1 Corinthians 4:12; 2 Corinthians 4:8-9;
Philippians 4:13; Hebrews 12:7

Where to take it

- Have you ever been in a situation where other people wanted you to fail but you pressed on? How did that make you feel?

- Master Chief Billy Sunday asks Carl, "What did your dad say to you to make you try so hard?" Carl replies, "To be the best." What are some words of wisdom that have inspired you and shaped your life? Who said them to you?

- The scene shows Carl Brashear facing impossible odds under water. Share what you were thinking and feeling as you watched this scene.

- Jesus faced opposition against religious leaders. What would have happened if Jesus didn't follow through and complete his ultimate purpose?

- Carl Brashear was the first African-American master diver. Is there anything that you desire to be the first to do?

- Carl is inspired and encouraged by the words and the example of his father. What words of encouragement has your heavenly father given to help you in your life?

Minority Report

Trailer

Do you relive your past
over and over?

The movie sci-fi/adventure, PG-13

Chief John Anderton (Tom Cruise) is in charge of the Justice Department's elite
Pre-Crime unit. In Washington, D.C., in the year 2054, premeditated murder
no longer exists. Using the talents of three psychics who are able to envision
murders before they occur, Chief Anderton and his team can stop a crime
before it happens. John's professional career is successful, but his personal life
has been crumbling since his son was abducted and his marriage,
subsequently, falls apart. When the Pre-Crime system predicts that he will
murder someone in the next 36 hours, John is on the run in order to discover
what his future will be.

This clip (3 minutes)

▶ **Start** / 0:17:00 / Camera pans rows of pictures.

■ **Stop** / 0:20:00 / John inhales one of his drugs to
help him forget.

At the end of every day, John goes home to an empty house and relives
memories of happier times with his family. As he illuminates a 3-D video of his
son, John listens to his son's voice and replays conversations they had together.
He uses drugs to deaden the pain as he tries to linger in a life that is no more.

By the Book

Psalm 34:18; 42:5; 119:28; Isaiah 43:18; Lamentations 3:32; John 16:20

Where to take it

? John misses his son, Sean. He takes drugs while he relives a moment in time when his boy was with him. Do you do anything to numb your pain?

? We tend to look at drugs and alcohol as the "biggies" when it comes to escaping pain and life; however, there are other escapes such as food, television, isolation, shopping, and many more. What do you do to keep from feeling pain? How do you distance yourself from your problems?

? What are some healthy (and biblical) ways to deal with the pain and problems of this world?

? What memories do you get stuck in?

? How do you think God feels about the losses we experience?

? What does it mean to have "ghosts" of your past? How do you cope with or deal with them and proceed to live a life of purpose?

Trailer

Are you afraid of the boogey-man?

The movie — family/animation, G

Mike Wazowski (voiced by Billy Crystal) and Sully (voiced by John Goodman) are the star employees of Monsters, Inc., a company whose business is to capture children's screams and use them as the energy source for their city. Such a job is not without risks, however. When the monsters sneak through the closets, there is the possibility they will actually have physical contact with the children they are trying to scare—a dangerous prospect that frightens the monsters. When a young girl named Boo (voiced by Mary Gibbs) mistakes Sully for a big, furry kitty, she follows him back to Monstropolis, and the entire monster world is thrown into turmoil. Sully and Mike must find a way to get the terrifying toddler back through her closet door before the decontamination squad discovers them, which would ruin their reputation. They are surprised to find that children are not as deadly as they had been told and that there is a far greater power source than a scream.

This clip (just under 2 minutes)

▶ **Start** / 0:01:32 / "Goodnight, sweetheart."

■ **Stop** / 0:03:14 / "Simulation terminated. Simulation terminated."

A little boy is tucked in bed and wished a good night by his parents. When the bedroom lights go off, the smallest of sounds become suspicious and regular objects seem to take irregular forms. Did he hear a creak in the closet? Is there something under the bed? Well...yes...there actually is a monster in the room, but he is only training for a future position at Monsters, Inc.

By the Book

Proverbs 3:24; 14:26; Isaiah 8:13; Lamentations 3:57; Matthew 10:28; Luke 12:6-7; 2 Timothy 1:7

Where to take it

? What are the things in life you fear—your "boogey-men"?

? What do you do to stomp out your fears (e.g., turn on all the lights in your house, check under the bed, check the closets, etc.)?

? What did you fear when you were younger? Do you still have these fears?

? How would your friends describe you: fearless or fearful?

? How powerful a force is fear in your life?

? Ralph Waldo Emerson writes, "Do the thing we fear, and the death of fear is certain." What does this mean to you?

? Is fear sometimes an excuse for not living the life God has called us to live?

? Read Proverbs 14:26, Isaiah 8:13, and Matthew 10:28. What do these passages say about fear?

117

Moonlight Mile

Trailer
It's time to come clean.

The movie   drama, PG-13

After the death of his fiancée, Diane, Joe Nast (Jake Gyllenhaal) finds himself living with his "would have been" in-laws, Ben and Jojo Floss (Dustin Hoffman and Susan Sarandon). Joe is confused about his future and about the role he should play in Ben and Jojo's family. Dutifully staying in their home and working as Ben's business partner, Joe tries to be a comfort to Diane's parents. However, he begins to feel trapped in a situation he doesn't want to be in, yet he can't seem to escape without revealing a secret about his relationship with Diane that he fears will devastate both Ben and Jojo.

This clip   [4 minutes]

▶ **Start** / 1:33:12 / "Joseph Nast. N-A-S-T."

■ **Stop** / 1:37:42 / Joe sighs and smiles after his confession.

During the trial of the man who killed Diane, the Flosses' lawyer (Holly Hunter) puts Joe on the witness stand with the hopes that his testimony will help their case. Joe tries to paint a picture that will make everything right for Ben and Jojo, but he is unable to manufacture any such story. Finally, Joe confesses the truth about Diane and about what she planned to tell her father the day she was shot. Although he doesn't like the reality that Diane will never come back, Joe realizes he must tell the truth about who she really was.

By the Book

Job 16:19; Psalm 51:6; Proverbs 3:3; 24:28; John 3:21; Ephesians 4:25;
Hebrews 13:7; James 1:22; 1 John 1:5-10

Where to take it

? Joe describes Diane as "strong, real, messed-up, and wickedly honest." If people were called to the witness stand to testify about you, how would they describe your character?

? When your life is over, how do you want to be remembered?

? Joe says, "The truth is hard. Sometimes it looks so wrong." What might this statement mean?

? What do you think Joe means when he says that the good ones live in the truth?

? Scripture talks a lot about truth. Read Psalm 51:6, Proverbs 3:3, and John 3:21. Pick one of these verses that you can apply to your character. Which one did you choose and why?

? Is there any "truth" that needs to be revealed about your life? What encouragement and direction does 1 John 1:5-10 give you about confessing that truth?

? God's Word is also truth. What do Hebrews 13:7 and James 1:22 instruct you to do with this truth?

The Mothman Prophecies

Trailer

How does evil lurk in this world?

The movie — drama, PG-13

Washington Post reporter John Klein (Richard Gere) is having a difficult time moving on with his life after losing his wife to a rare cancer. Two years later, he sets out late at night to drive to Virginia for an interview with the governor, but he inexplicably has car trouble 400 miles away in Point Pleasant, West Virginia. Over the next few days, John discovers that there have been numerous local sightings of a large moth-shaped creature. He talks to a couple of residents who have been given prophetic information by this entity about future disasters that do, in fact, happen. Just as troubling to John is the description of the creature given by those who have seen it; it is similar to a creature his wife sketched before she passed away. He then becomes obsessed with uncovering the meaning of these signs.

This clip (just under 4 minutes)

▶ **Start** / 0:54:08 / fade in on exterior of motel.

⏹ **Stop** / 0:58:30 / "I've been asleep since nine o'clock."

When the mysterious being makes contact with John and another Point Pleasant resident, Gordon (Will Patton), he identifies himself as Indrid Cold. One night, Gordon calls John to tell him that Indrid Cold is at his house. John asks to speak to him and tries to test him by asking a series of questions. John is unnerved by what the voice on the phone seems to know about him.

By the Book

Job 1:7; Psalm 23:4; 121:7; Luke 10:19; Romans 16:20; Ephesians 6:12;
1 Peter 5:8; 1 John 5:19

Where to take it

? Describe a time when you
encountered a phenomenon that you
just could not explain.

? Read Job 1:7 and 1 John 5:19. What
do these passages say about the
power of evil in this world?

? Do you believe there are forces in
this world trying to harm us? What
does 1 Peter 5:8 say about this?

? How do you think evil can "play"
with us?

? Read Psalm 121:7 and Luke 10:19. How can we be equipped to fight the
enemy of our souls?

? John asks Indrid Cold what he looks like, and Indrid replies, "It depends
on who's looking." What do you think that means? How might this be
similar to the ways Satan works? How does Satan use personal issues and
insecurities to confuse and deceive us?

The movie drama/musical, PG-13

It's 1899 and Christian (Ewan McGregor) has defied his father's warnings; he's moved to a seedy section of Paris so he can experience life and find his inspiration to write about love. While he's there, Christian gets mixed up with a rag-tag bunch of bohemians who want him to write a musical play for the legendary nightclub, dance hall, and brothel—the Moulin Rouge. The star of the Moulin Rouge is Satine (Nicole Kidman). The owner, Zilder (Jim Broadbent), wants Satine to get a wealthy Duke (Richard Roxburgh) to pay to transform the club into a legitimate theater and finance the first show. However, the Duke will finance the show only if Satine's affections are included in the deal. When Satine falls in love with Christian, a dangerous love triangle develops, and in the end, she must decide if love is strong enough to conquer all.

This clip (just under 4 minutes)

▶ **Start** / 0:48:35 / "Silly me. To think that you could fall in love with someone like me."

■ **Stop** / 0:53:00 / Fireworks in the sky with a moon singing.

When Satine first meets Christian, she thinks he is a wealthy Duke and is more than willing to fall for him. Later, she learns that he is only a poor writer. Christian climbs up to her balcony and tries to convince Satine that love is all they need, but Satine is not so easily persuaded. The world she lives in is more about survival than about love. Through a medley of songs, Christian sets out to talk her into giving their relationship a chance...in the name of love. Although Satine wants to believe the things he is singing to her, she tries to keep her guard up with him. Gradually, her walls crumble, and she takes a chance on the love-struck poet.

By the Book

1 Corinthians 13:1-13; 16:14; Colossians 3:14; 1 Peter 4:8; 1 John 4:7-11; 2 John 1:6

Where to take it

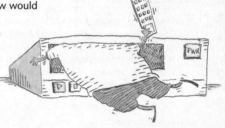

❓ Define *love*. How is love defined in 1 John 4:10 and 2 John 1:6?

❓ Have you ever known people who guard themselves? People who won't let you get close to them or know what they are feeling?

❓ Do you think true love exists? How would you describe it?

❓ What do you think is necessary for a relationship to last a lifetime?

❓ Why do you think feelings change in relationships?

❓ What does the statement "love is a choice" mean to you?

❓ 1 Corinthians 13 is known as the "love" chapter in the Bible. Read the attributes of love listed there. Which do you think you possess? Which ones are the most difficult for you to live?

Mr. Deeds

Trailer

How much "abuse" do you take from others?

The movie — comedy, PG-13

Longfellow Deeds (Adam Sandler) is a likeable guy from Mandrake Falls, New Hampshire, who is perfectly content writing greeting cards, delivering pizza, and performing good deeds for the people in his small town. When he gets a visit from the top executives of Blake Media, he learns that he, the only living heir of the late Preston Blake, stands to inherit $40 billion. He travels to New York City to finalize a deal that, unbeknownst to Deeds, will put control of his late uncle's corporation into the hands of CEO Chuck Cedar (Peter Gallagher) and General Counsel Cecil Anderson (Erick Avari). Their only intent is to sell it for their personal profit. Cedar and Anderson don't realize, however, the impact this small-town man can have, not only on the big city, but on their big plans as well.

This clip — (about 2 minutes)

▶ **Start** / 0:21:16 / "That's Hawaiian Punch!"

⏹ **Stop** / 0:23:23 / "There you go."

While Deeds is in New York City, arrangements are made for him to stay at his late uncle's home. The lavish apartment comes complete with serving staff, including a rather eccentric butler, Emilio (John Turturro). One morning, Emilio enters Deeds' bedroom to help him get dressed for the day. When Emilio offers to change Deeds' socks, Deeds shows Emilio his right foot, blackened and numbed by frostbite. Deeds challenges Emilio to jump on his foot as hard as he can, assuring him that he cannot feel any pain. The butler is at first reluctant to inflict any abuse, but then he is drawn to the challenge of trying to get some response from the deadened foot.

By the Book

Matthew 5:11,43-44; Luke 6:31; John 13:34-35; Galatians 5:22; Ephesians 4:32; Hebrews 10:24

Where to take it

? Do you get picked on?

? Have people ever abused you verbally or with their actions? What effect did that have on you? What effect does it continue to have on you?

? Do you know anyone who has been physically abused? What do you imagine that person struggles with?

? In this clip, we see the butler beat on Deeds' deadened foot. Have you become numb to someone in your life who treats you badly? Why do you tolerate any type of abuse?

? What does the Bible teach us about how we should treat one another?

My Big Fat Greek Wedding

Trailer
Love can hurt...literally.

The movie comedy, PG

Toula (Nia Vardalos) is unmarried and has a family who will not let her forget it. Her Greek culture teaches Greek girls that they have three purposes in life: to marry a Greek man, to have Greek babies, and to feed everybody until death. While the rest of her family has followed this custom, Toula is 30 years old with no real prospects for marriage, so she decides to make some changes in her life. When she does find a man she loves, he is not Greek. Their love will not only have to conquer all, but it will have to take on her very loving, very quirky, and very Greek family.

This clip (just under 1 minute)

▶ **Start** / 0:26:04 / Toula sits at computer typing.

■ **Stop** / 0:27:31 / "Found them."

Toula is working at a travel agency answering phones when Ian Miller (John Corbett) sees her and tries to impress her by doing funny things outside her work window. This only proves painful as he bumps into an old woman who beats him with her handbag. Risking further embarrassment, Ian goes in to talk to Toula. She, then, makes a fool of herself, too.

By the Book

Genesis 2:18,24; Proverbs 18:22; 31:10; Song of Solomon 2:16;
1 Corinthians 13:1-13; Ephesians 5:33; Hebrews 13:4

Where to take it

(?) Describe a time when you saw someone you just had to meet. Are you glad you did? Is your life better for it?

(?) In this scene, Toula and Ian try to impress each other with rather painful results. Can you describe a time when you tried to impress someone but ended up looking like a fool?

(?) Scripture describes love in 1 Corinthians 13. Which of these qualities do you see in yourself and in your relationships?

(?) What do you think are qualities necessary for a long-lasting marriage?

(?) What values are you not willing to compromise when you choose to marry?

Do you have a "panic room"?

The movie   thriller, R

Recently divorced, Meg Altman (Jodie Foster) is trying to start a new life with her daughter Sarah (Kristen Stewart). Meg purchases a huge Manhattan brownstone once owned by an eccentric millionaire. This home includes a "panic room" that is reinforced by concrete walls and three inches of steel, creating an impenetrable fortress. This space is also equipped with a separate ventilation system, phone line, and surveillance monitors, as it is intended to be the ultimate security device against home invasion. When three burglars (Jared Leto, Forest Whitaker, and Dwight Yoakam) break into Meg's apartment, she dives into the panic room, sealing herself and her daughter inside. What these men have come for, however, cannot be found in the rest of the house— it's in the panic room.

This clip   (about 2 minutes)

▶ **Start** / 0:6:00 / "...and we emerge in the master suite."

■ **Stop** / 0:8:35 / "I know they'll take the asking price."

Meg gets the tour of the house and discovers the "panic room." The real estate agent takes Meg inside the room, shows her the special features, tells her why it was built, and demonstrates how to use it. When the agent activates the steel door to close them inside the room, Meg is shaken and asks to be let out. She is uncomfortable with what the room represents, even though it is meant to be a place of safety in times of trouble.

By the Book

Deuteronomy 31:6; Psalm 23:4; 27:4-6; 61:3; 91; 121:7-8; Proverbs 18:10;
2 Thessalonians 3:3; 1 John 4:18

Where to take it

? What do you do when you panic?

? Discuss your biggest fears.

? Where do you go to feel safe? Describe
the place or the person that
represents security to you.

? Read Psalm 27:4-6, Psalm 91, and
Proverbs 18:10. Do you think of
God as a "safe place"? What do
these verses say about God as a
place of refuge?

? As seen in this clip, the panic room
is designed to keep the enemy out
and the people inside protected.
When we spend time in solitude
and in God's Word, what are some
things God gives us to keep the
enemy at bay?

Pearl Harbor

Trailer
What life lessons can we learn from history?

The movie drama, PG-13

Rafe (Ben Affleck) and Danny (Josh Hartnett) are two lifelong friends who become pilots in the U.S. Army Air Corps during a time when much of the world is at war. Both men have great plans for their lives, both fall in love with the same woman, Evelyn (Kate Beckinsale), and both find their friendship threatened not only by the events of war but by the choices they make. Then, December 7, 1941, dawns and everyone's world is changed. The Japanese launch a surprise attack on the Pacific Fleet of the U.S. forces at Pearl Harbor. The ferocious bombing is devastating to the unprepared Naval station and to a country that thought it could stay out of the war. Rafe, Evelyn, and Danny are all in the middle of the events at Pearl Harbor that day, and the two men must put their feud aside to join the battle to defend their country.

This clip (just under 3 minutes)

▶ **Start** / beginning of 2nd VHS tape or 2nd DVD / "Is it true men are still trapped inside the Arizona?"

■ **Stop** / 0:02:55 / "Do not tell me it cannot be done."

President Franklin D. Roosevelt convenes his cabinet to discuss the status of and response to the Pearl Harbor attack. He tells them that America has just learned a difficult lesson; we are not invincible. Forcefully, he declares to his military leaders that he wants to strike back with fierceness at the heart of Japan. In response, all he gets are explanations of what can't be done. Looking into the eyes of his staff, he senses the spirit of defeat. The president then takes a daring step to illustrate that he is not going to let any obstacle, especially fear, deter his nation from victory.

By the Book

Matthew 19:26; Philippians 3:14; 4:13; 1 Timothy 6:12; 2 Timothy 1:7; 1 John 5:3-4

Where to take it

? The president addresses his men on the situation with Japan: "They seemed inferior. The enemy has taken us by surprise." Describe a time in your spiritual walk when you thought yourself immune to a certain sin only to find the enemy had found another way to defeat you.

? President Roosevelt admonishes his leaders: "Does anyone in this room think that victory is possible without facing danger? We are at war!" How willing are you to fight for victory in your walk with Christ? What do you think it takes to have such victory? What are the hardships that you face?

? Roosevelt reveals why he believes God put him in a wheelchair. What is your "handicap?" Why do you think God allows you to endure this affliction?

? When other Christians look into your eyes, do they see defeat by the world, or do they see perseverance and a desire to keep fighting the good fight?

? What do you think and/or feel when you see the president struggle to stand on his crippled legs in order to show the rest of the men in the room that they should not accept defeat?

? Have you ever encouraged someone to keep walking in the way of faith? What did you say to strengthen him or her?

? What do you think God's purpose is for you?

? Read Philippians 3:14 and 1 Timothy 6:12. What do these passages say about pressing on and not giving up?

The Princess Diaries

Trailer

What will you choose to be?

The movie comedy, G

Mia Thermopolis (Anne Hathaway) is trying to survive her sophomore year of high school. She is clumsy and awkward and longs to remain invisible so she can avoid the embarrassment she constantly brings upon herself. When she is united with a grandmother (Julie Andrews) she's never known, Mia gets the unbelievable news that her deceased father was the Prince of Genovia, which makes her next in line as heir. She has only two weeks to prepare for her presentation at the royal ball. In those two weeks, her world and her friendships are turned upside down as the news of her identity is leaked to the press. She is no longer invisible. As the evening of the big event approaches, Mia must decide if she can set aside her personal fears and desires to take on the responsibilities of her position.

This clip (just under 3 minutes)

▶ **Start** / 1:41:53 / "I'm really no good at speechmaking."

⏹ **Stop** / 1:44:39 / "Me."

Mia had decided to leave town and forget about the weight of ruling Genovia, but then she finds a note that her father wrote to her before he died. In the letter, he shares with Mia that courage is not the absence of fear but the knowledge that there is something more important than fear. The night of the ball, Mia dashes out into a rainstorm to get to the ceremony before the crown is handed over to her cousin. She confesses to the guests that she tried to run away but then realized that the important part of being a princess is not what it does for her, but what it enables her to do for others.

By the Book

Matthew 20:28; 26:39; Luke 9:23-25; Philippians 2:3-5

Where to take it

? In her speech, Mia talks about how many times a day she says the word "I." How many times during the day do you say "I"? During the day, when are you least focused on yourself?

? Mia professes that when people put their thoughts into action, they can change the world. What can you do to make a difference in your community?

? What is larger than yourself that you think is important enough to commit your life to?

? Why do you think the ministry of Jesus has lasted for thousands of years and affected millions?

? Read Matthew 20:28. How did Jesus view himself?

? Read Luke 9:23-25. What did Jesus say about how we should view ourselves?

? If you had the opportunity to rule a country, knowing all the responsibility it would demand, would you take it? Why or why not?

? Read Matthew 26:39. Jesus was in the garden of Gethsemane wrestling with his choice to sacrifice himself for us. Share your thoughts as you read this.

133

The Recruit

Why are you here?

The movie — thriller, PG-13

James Clayton (Colin Farrell) is a brilliant and confident computer graduate from M.I.T. His talents catch the highly-experienced eye of CIA recruiter, Walter Burke (Al Pacino). Clayton is a natural and quickly moves to the head of his class at the CIA training grounds, known as "the farm." During an especially grueling operation, Clayton breaks down and is dropped from the program. But in the CIA, nothing is what it seems. Burke uses the opportunity to offer James the highly-coveted position of NOC, an undercover spy within the agency, in order to root out any moles working in the CIA. This assignment leads James down a dangerous road of deceit and betrayal as he must discern who can and who can't be trusted.

This clip — (about 2 minutes)

▶ **Start** / 0:18:32 / "Ladies and gentlemen, my name is Dennis Slayne."

◼ **Stop** / 0:20:37 / "Nothing is what it seems."

Special Agent Burke talks to the new recruits about why they are at the farm. He tells them that the CIA is not a life of riches and fame. Burke also explains that the nature of the agency is such that none of their successes will be widely recognized, much less rewarded; however, when they fail, everyone will know. Burke informs the recruits that they are there because of what they believe and because of their willingness to act on those beliefs.

By the Book

Proverbs 14:12; 28:10; Isaiah 5:20; Matthew 7:13; Ephesians 6:13; Titus 2:7-9

Where to take it

(?) The recruits are asked, "Why are you here?" How would you answer this question if it were asked about your life?

(?) Walter Burke lists fame, money, and sex as reasons not to be a part of the elite organization. As Christians, what do we need to be willing to give up in order to seek God's kingdom first?

(?) Burke states, "Our failures are known, our successes are not." How might this also be true in the world of Christianity?

(?) Burke tells the agents, "I think the reason we are all sitting in this room is because we believe. We believe in good and evil, and we choose good. We believe in right and wrong, and we choose right." How closely are your choices tied to what you believe? Describe a time when you made a good decision and a time when you made a bad decision. Explain the beliefs that motivated each decision.

(?) The Bible specifically delineates right and wrong, good and evil. Read Proverbs 14:12, Isaiah 5:20, and Matthew 7:13. In what ways do you try to hide in the "gray" areas of life or rationalize what is clearly stated in the Bible?

(?) What forms do you think evil takes in our world? What are the most obvious forms of evil? What are some of the more subtle forms?

Remember the Titans

Trailer
Unleash the leader inside.

The movie   drama, PG

When Herman Boone (Denzel Washington), a black man, is named the head coach at a newly integrated high school, the news comes as quite a shock to everyone, including the current and much beloved Coach Bill Yoast (Will Patton), who is white. The two coaches, whose personalities are as different as their skin colors, must work together to unify a team of untrusting and fearful black and white students. Rising to the occasion, the two men force the team members to get to know one another, to respect each other, and to learn to become winners together. The result is contagious and has a profound effect on the town.

This clip   (just under 5 minutes)

▶ **Start** / 0:29:15 / "All right, man, listen. I'm Gerry, you're Julius."

■ **Stop** / 0:34:00 / "And maybe learn to play this game like men."

Reluctant to follow their coach's demand to get to know each other, but unwilling to suffer additional practice time for not doing so, Gerry (Ryan Hurst) approaches Julius (Wood Harris) to share a few facts about themselves in order to show the coach they got to know each other. However, the two end up in a heated and honest discussion about what they think of each other. Gerry confronts Julius about his selfishness and laziness on the field. In return, Gerry gets a bit of truth as Julius explains how his leadership only serves his white friends and none of the others on the team. Early the next morning, Coach Boone takes the team for a run they will never forget. He leads them to the field where the Battle of Gettysburg was fought. Boone explains to the young men that lives were lost on this battlefield because of racial hatred and division, and he tells them to listen to the graves of these dead soldiers so they can understand the legacy as well as the cost of hate and separation.

By the Book

Psalm 133:1; Proverbs 10:12,17; 28:16; Matthew 7:12; Luke 22:26; Philippians 2:1-2

Where to take it

(?) Julius tells Gerry that attitude reflects leadership. How is this true?

(?) Which is more important for a leader to have, character or charisma?

(?) What do you think are the top three essential qualities of a leader?

(?) Gerry calls Julius "a waste of God-given talent." What would you say a waste of God-given talent means?

(?) Boone takes the team to Gettysburg and discusses the soldiers who died there. What similar battlegrounds, internationally and in your backyard, still exist today? What battlegrounds still exist amongst your friends?

(?) The coach challenges his players when he says, "You may not like each other, but you will learn to respect each other." How is this possible?

(?) Boone also says, "Listen to these dead men's souls and take a lesson from the dead." What are some lessons you have learned from those who have passed away?

The Rookie

Trailer

When you got it...use it.

The movie — drama, G

Jim Morris (Dennis Quaid) grew up loving and playing baseball, and like any kid, he dreamed of one day making it to the major leagues. When he did get his opportunity, a shoulder injury sidelined him, and he put aside his dreams of playing major league baseball. He marries, has a family, and works as a high-school science teacher and baseball coach. With his dream still lingering in his soul, he takes a bet that will change his life.

This clip (just under 7 minutes)

- ▶ **Start** / 0:31:17 / "Anybody want to tell me how we lost that game?"

- ■ **Stop** / 0:38:10 / Speed limit sign changes from 76 to 96.

When Coach Morris questions his high-school baseball team about why they lost a game, the team members are honest, saying they lack motivation. When Coach Morris tries to give them a pep talk about not quitting and committing to accomplishing greater goals together, his speech gets turned back at him. The team starts asking him why he gave up on the major leagues. The young men make their coach an offer: if they make it to the district championship, Morris must try out again for the big leagues. Morris remembers his dream well but wonders if he still has what it takes to make it happen.

By the Book

Proverbs 18:16; 23:18; Matthew 25:14-30; Luke 1:37; Romans 12:6-8;
1 Corinthians 12:4-11; 2 Corinthians 8:11; James 1:12

Where to take it

Do you know someone who is wasting his or her God-given talents? Why do you think people waste their God-given abilities?

Have you ever taken risks in order to see what you could accomplish? What happened?

Coach Morris challenges his team to hold onto their season and not give up; he challenges the players to put their hearts into something that will benefit them in the long run. What have you stopped believing in or working toward that, perhaps, you need to start believing in and working toward again?

Romans 12:6-8 describes the different types of gifts that God gives his people such as prophecy, service, teaching, encouragement, giving, leadership, and mercy. Do any of these jump out at you as gifts you may have? How could you apply these gifts?

Read the parable of the talents in Matthew 25:14-30. What do you think about the servants' use of the talents given to them? What do you think about the master's response?

When you are 50, what do you want to see as you reflect on your life?

Serendipity

Trailer

Is it destiny or an accident?

The movie — romantic comedy, PG-13

While Christmas shopping in New York City, Jonathon Trager (John Cusack) and Sara Thomas (Kate Beckinsale) meet at Bloomingdale's as they both reach for the same pair of gloves. They laugh about the encounter and go their separate ways but run into each other again later that night. Was this meant to be or was it just coincidence? They enjoy spending the evening together, and they decide to exchange information so they can contact one another. Agreeing that if they are meant to be together it will happen without their intervention, though, Sara writes her phone number in a book that she will sell to a used-book store and Jonathon writes his number on a five dollar bill that he plans to spend. They decide that if either one of them ends up with the other's phone number, they were meant to be together.

This clip (just under 5 minutes)

▶ **Start** / 0:04:39 / "This will work though. This is quite a coffee."

■ **Stop** / 0:09:36 / "This one's climbing the charts."

Jonathan and Sara sit at a table in the Serendipity café talking about fate. Sara believes that there is no such thing as an accident but that signs will guide us if we know how to read them. The two are honest about their current relationships but are also intrigued by one another. After leaving the café, they say goodbye only to end up meeting again that same night. Delightfully surprised to see one another, they take advantage of the fortunate accident and go ice skating in Rockefeller Center.

By the Book

Proverbs 16:9; Isaiah 55:9; Jeremiah 29:11; Matthew 10:29-31; Romans 8:28

Where to take it

? In this clip, two strangers meet, end up liking one another, and say that it was meant to happen. Does this occur in real life, or this just a Hollywood fable?

? How much of what happens in this world and in your life do you believe is controlled by God? If your answer is less than 100 percent, what other forces, if any, do you think are at work?

? Some people believe in "divine appointments," claiming that God has a way of getting certain people to meet at certain times. What do you think about this?

? What do Jeremiah 29:11, Matthew 10:29-31, and Romans 8:28 say about God's interest and activity in the details of our lives?

? Do you think God gives us signs that offer direction? How does he do this?

? Define *soul mate*. What do you think are the main ingredients of true compatibility?

? Do you think there are several different people in this world who you could love and commit to for the rest of your life, or do you think that there is just one person on the planet who you are destined to be with?

? Describe a time when you think you saw "serendipity" in action.

141

Shallow Hal

Trailer

Should a person's appearance mask inner beauty?

The movie comedy, PG-13

Hal Larson (Jack Black) was only nine years old when his father died, but before he died, he gave Hal advice for finding the right woman. Following his father's last words, Hal grows up to be a superficial guy who is obsessed with physical beauty. He hangs out in clubs and seeks women who are not interested in anything he has to offer. However, things change when Hal gets stuck in an elevator with "self-help guru" Tony Robbins who hypnotizes him to see only a woman's inner beauty. After this meeting, Hal falls in love with Rosemary (Gwyneth Paltrow), a 300-pound woman. He is the only one who sees her as an extremely attractive woman, and he also discovers that she's kind, funny, and smart. Hal's equally shallow friend, Mauricio (Jason Alexander), cannot believe what has happened and tries to find a way to reverse Hal's perception. When the hypnosis is reversed and Hal sees Rosemary as she really is, he must decide what is truly important.

This clip (just under 1 minute)

▶ **Start** / 0:43:17 / "No, that's just it. I've never been close enough to anybody to get burned."

■ **Stop** / 0:44:45 / Image fades.

After spending the day with her, Hal walks Rosemary back to her apartment. They begin to talk about relationships, and Hal asks Rosemary about all the boyfriends he is convinced she must have had. Everything Hal says to Rosemary indicates he thinks she is beautiful, but she is uncomfortable with the way he talks to her. When she outlines what she thinks are her qualities, being pretty definitely isn't on the list. Hal doesn't understand why she is getting upset, as he is only communicating what he sees.

By the Book

Proverbs 31:30; Matthew 5:8; Luke 10:27; 1 Corinthians 13:1-7;
1 Timothy 1:5; 2 Timothy 2:22; 1 Peter 3:3-4

Where to take it

- List a few qualities a person of the opposite sex must have to interest you. Do you possess the attributes that you want to see in someone else?

- Do you agree with the statement, "Don't look for the right person, be the right person"? Why or why not?

- Do your standards for a friend differ from your standards for someone you would date? Why or why not?

- Why do you think most people in our culture believe it is important to be physically attractive? What traits are more essential than beauty?

- Watch the scene again and listen to Rosemary list what she thinks are her characteristics. Can you relate to what she says?

- Can you take a compliment?

- Think about some men and women in the Old Testament. What attributes did they value and strive to attain?

- Girls: What do you want guys to know about you? What do you want them to see in you?

- Guys: What do you want girls to know about you? What do you want them to see in you?

Shrek

The movie   animation, PG

Shrek (voiced by Mike Myers) is an ugly, green, ill-tempered ogre who enjoys living alone in his swamp. One night, some fairytale characters are unwillingly relocated to his front yard by the very short, very power-hungry Lord Farquaad (voiced by John Lithgow). Farquaad is in the process of establishing a kingdom for himself but can't be officially crowned a king until he marries a princess. Shrek makes a deal with Farquaad to rescue the lovely Princess Fiona (voiced by Cameron Diaz) from the dragon-guarded tower where she is trapped if Farquaad will get the fairy-tale characters off his property. Shrek and his sidekick, Donkey (voiced by Eddie Murphy), free Fiona and escort her back to marry Farquaad. On the way, the Princess and Shrek begin to fall in love with each other. Could a princess ever love an ogre, or is Shrek destined to be alone forever?

This clip   (7 minutes)

▶ **Start** / 1:15:25 / "Shrek, wait, wait! Wait a minute! You wanna do this right, don't you?"

■ **Stop** / 1:22:55 / "Aww, I was hoping this would be a happy ending."

Donkey tells Shrek that he has misunderstood Fiona and that she really does care for him, and Shrek races to the church to stop Princess from marrying Farquaad. Watching the sun as it sets in the sky, Fiona rushes the ceremony, hoping that a kiss with Farquaad will break the spell and allow her to remain a lovely princess. When Shrek stops the wedding and confesses how he really feels about her, Fiona is willing to reveal what happens to her when the sun goes down. When she finally kisses the one she really loves, her true self is revealed.

By the Book

1 Samuel 16:7; Proverbs 31:30; Mark 6:34; John 7:24; 2 Corinthians 4:16;
1 John 4:9-11,15-19

Where to take it

? How do you define true love? Do you think most people marry for true love?

? Why do you think our society places so much emphasis on external traits rather than on internal ones?

? What three inner qualities do you hope people find beautiful in you?

? Read Mark 6:34. How did Christ show love to others?

? Fiona's curse had forced her to live two lives—one by day when she felt she was beautiful enough to be seen, and one by night when she would hide herself from everyone. Can you relate to Fiona? How do you hide the parts of you that you think are ugly?

? What does it mean to "take love's true form"? Read 1 John 4:9-11. What does this passage say is love's true form?

? Fiona thought that after her curse was broken and her true love was revealed, she would be "beautiful." Her true love tells her that she is beautiful. Read 1 John 4:15-19. Who in your life sees you as you truly are, even the parts that are not so pretty, and still loves you completely?

The Siege

Is terrorism a part of life?

The movie   action, R

When Middle Eastern terrorists unleash a chain of escalating attacks on New York City, FBI special agent Anthony Hubbard (Denzel Washington) and his partner, Frank Haddad (Tony Shalhoub), are assigned the task of rooting out the terror cells. In their investigation, the two men cross paths with a CIA operative, Elise Kraft (Annette Bening), who knows much more about the terrorist activity than she is willing to admit. When the FBI can't stop the violence, the president authorizes the use of military force. General William Devereaux (Bruce Willis) and his troops lock down the borough of Brooklyn and begin to imprison its Arab-American citizens. Hubbard must fight both Kraft and the General to find the answers necessary to prevent any more destruction.

This clip (about 6 minutes)

▶ **Start** / 0:18:51 / "Three men, definitely armed...."

⏹ **Stop** / 0:25:25 / Cops rush to scene of explosion in slow motion.

Hubbard rushes to the scene of a bus full of hostages; there are reports that a man with a bomb is onboard. Hubbard and Haddad begin to negotiate with the hijacker for the release of the passengers. As news crews and helicopters continue to arrive at the scene, Kraft advises Hubbard to do something drastic to end the situation because if a terrorist is in control of the crisis, the media attention will only encourage him to do the worst. Hubbard ignores her warnings and even makes some progress with the suspect before the terrorist plays his final card.

By the Book

Genesis 25:12-18; 1 Chronicles 1:28; Proverbs 24:6; Ecclesiastes 3:8; Isaiah 2:4; Acts 20:28

Where to take it

? What is a religious war?

? Read Genesis 25:12-18 and 1 Chronicles 1:28. When and where did conflicts between different religions begin? Does it amaze you that some of the same countries have been fighting for so long? Will we always have to be on guard against terrorism?

? Why do you think one nation believes God wants suicide bombings while another nation views it as murder?

? Read Ecclesiastes 3:8 and Isaiah 2:4. What does God have to say about war in these verses?

? If we had as much fervor for God and Christ as some people do for their religious causes, do you think we'd see more people come to know God? Why or why not?

? How have the events of 9/11 changed our world? How have they changed you? What do you think is God's perspective on these events?

The movie thriller/drama, PG-13

Graham Hess (Mel Gibson), a single father and former clergyman, lives on a farm in rural Pennsylvania with his two children and his brother. Six months earlier, his wife was killed in a gruesome car accident. Since then, Graham has walked away from his church and everything connected to his faith in God. He doesn't allow anyone to refer to him as "Father," and he won't pray. When his two children discover a massive crop circle on their farm, Graham assumes it is a stunt pulled by local pranksters. As additional circles start showing up all around the world, however, he realizes that more extreme powers are at work, and his faith, or lack thereof, is tested.

This clip [5 minutes]

▶ **Start** / 0:41:09 / Close-up of two glasses with water.

■ **Stop** / 0:46:09 / Fades as family sits on the couch.

Graham and his younger brother, Merrill (Joaquin Phoenix), sit on the couch discussing the nature of divine intervention. Graham tells Merrill that there are two kinds of people—those who believe in miracles and those who believe in luck. Those who believe in miracles are convinced that someone is watching out for them; therefore, they have hope. The ones who believe in luck know they are on their own, and when events occur which they cannot explain, they are fearful. Believing that there is no such thing as coincidence and God has a reason for everything, Merrill says that he is the first kind of person. Graham, on the other hand, tells Merrill that there is no one watching out for us and we are on our own.

By the Book

Isaiah 55:8-9; Jeremiah 29:11; Matthew 6:25-34; Romans 8:28,38; Revelation 21:1-4

Where to take it

? What do you think the end of the world will look like? What does Scripture say about end times?

? Graham divides people in two groups:
  1. Those who think everything happens for a reason, and God is in control.
  2. Those who think everything happens by chance, luck, or coincidence.
In which group would you place yourself? Why? Do you think there is any "middle ground"?

? Read Matthew 6:25-34. Can this be interpreted to mean that God takes care of every little detail, and that there is no such thing as chance? If so, why do bad things happen?

? Do you believe in miracles? Describe any experience you have had for which there is no explanation other than "it was a God-thing."

? Graham believes that no one is watching out for us and we are on our own. Do you feel this way? Why?

? The basis of this conversation between the brothers is that what we believe shapes who we are, what we do, and how we view what happens to us. Does what you believe shape who you are, what you do, and how you view what happens to you?

Singles

The movie — comedy, PG-13

Several 20-somethings who live in the same Seattle apartment building are trying to find their paths in the world and in their relationships. While some are just stumbling into dating, some are dating with a definite plan—to locate their soul mates. Others are ready to give up on finding the right person. Through the beginnings, the fears, the risks, the failures, and the endings, these young adults press on in their journeys: discovering true love or choosing to stay single.

This clip (about 1 minute)

▶ **Start** / 0:08:35 / Black and white picture that reads, "Have Fun. Stay Single."

■ **Stop** / 0:10:08 / "I was eight!"

Steve Dunne (Campbell Scott) is talking about his latest break-up. Although he knew the relationship wasn't right, he says he kept it going anyway. Steve expresses the pain that comes with a break-up and how much more difficult it is when the other person quickly moves on to someone else. Steve holds up a postcard of two people kissing and says how he wishes love could be that simple.

...clip continued

(**Warning:** There is language about sex in this clip.)

You can continue this clip, but Steve does talk about sex—he remembers the time when his mother sent him to the doctor's office to learn about it. The content may be suitable only for mature audiences.

By the Book

Ecclesiastes 11:9; Jeremiah 29:11; Romans 12:1; 1 Timothy 4:12; Hebrews 13:4

Where to take it

(?) Have you ever been in a relationship that you and the other person knew needed to end? Have you ever had a break-up that left you sad and depressed?

(?) What do you think single people endure when they want to get married but cannot find the right person?

(?) What does Hebrews 13:4 say about marriage? What does Ecclesiastes 11:9 say about youth and being single?

(?) What came to your mind when Steve Dunn held up the picture of the couple kissing? Do you hope you can find that type of romance? Do you think there are relationships that are that "simple"? Why or why not?

(?) What are the advantages of being single? What are the advantages of being in a committed relationship?

(?) What are some things you want to accomplish before getting married?

(?) Do you know someone or are you someone who always wants a boyfriend/girlfriend? Why do you think these people feel this way? Do you think it is a problem for someone always to want to have a boyfriend/girlfriend? Why or why not?

(?) "To meet the right person, you have to be the right person." What do you think this statement means?

(?) In the clip, Steve talks about some advice his dad gave him. What advice have you gotten from your parents about relationships?

Trailer

Choices can either make us
or break us.

The movie · thriller/sci-fi, PG-13

Peter Parker (Tobey Maguire) is a normal teenage kid with normal teenage problems. He's got a crush on the girl next door, Mary Jane Watson (Kirsten Dunst); he likes science; and he gets picked on at school. While on a field trip, he gets bitten by a genetically-engineered spider. Peter awakens the next morning with super-strength, the ability to spin webs, and the capacity to sense when something is about to happen. These traits don't improve his social life, but he gradually gets to spend more time with Mary Jane (when he is not helping to rid the city of crime). His only other friend is Harry Osborn (James Franco), but it turns out that his friend's father, Norman Osborn (Willem Dafoe), is Spiderman's arch nemesis—the Green Goblin.

This clip (just under 3 minutes)

▶ **Start** / 1:40:42 / "Goblin, what have you done?"

■ **Stop** / 1:44:05 / "He's gonna make it."

The Green Goblin has kidnapped Mary Jane and set her on the highest point of Brooklyn Bridge. He has also severed the cable supporting a car full of kids in order to lure Spiderman into making a choice. Which one is most important to the superhero? Does he save his "love" or rescue the kids? The Green Goblin tells Spiderman that we are who we choose to be, and he forces Spiderman to think and act fast as he drops Mary Jane and the cable holding the car full of kids, and they begin to fall to their deaths.

By the Book

Deuteronomy 30:19-20; Joshua 24:15; Psalm 25:12; Proverbs 3:5-6;
Luke 12:48; 1 Peter 5:8

Where to take it

The main theme of the movie is "With great power comes great responsibility." How is this true in everyday life? Read Luke 12:48. In what ways is Jesus' statement similar to and/or different from the theme in *Spiderman?*

The Green Goblin tells Spiderman, "We are who we chose to be." What does this mean to you?

How do you think the choices you make today will affect your life in the future? What decisions that you made in your past continue to affect you now?

Spiderman must choose between the person he loves and the lives of innocent people. He ends up saving both. Talk about a time in your life when a decision you made didn't work out this well.

Do you ever feel like there is a "Green Goblin" intentionally messing up the choices you make? Do you believe Satan has tried to interfere when you have decisions to make? Discuss some of the ways Satan has tried to thwart you.

Are there times when you know you are making the right choices but you still experience setbacks and heartache? Why do you think this happens?

The Sum of All Fears

The movie   action/thriller, PG-13

In the early 1970s, an Israeli airplane carrying a nuclear bomb crashes in Syria. Years later, the unexploded bomb is dug up and sold on the black market to a small terrorist group. The terrorists plan to use the bomb and the political climate to open the door for a nuclear showdown between the U.S. and Russia. Jack Ryan (Ben Affleck) is a young CIA agent who becomes involved in the conflict because he is one of only a few people familiar with the relatively unknown man who has just become president of Russia. When a nuclear bomb levels the capital of Chechnya and tragedy strikes at the Super Bowl, the U.S. government is convinced that Russia's new leader is responsible. Jack knows that these events were the work of another enemy, but can he get the information to the right people in time?

This clip (just under 2 minutes)

▶ **Start** / 1:43:49 / Jack Ryan runs out of helicopter.

■ **Stop** / 1:45:38 / "He doesn't have to."

The terrorists have successfully manipulated the circumstances to escalate tensions between the U.S. and Russia, and nuclear war seems imminent. With very little time to deliver the information needed to stop a war that will wipe the world's two most powerful nations off the map, Jack must fight to prove that the information he has is the truth and that the forces at work are terrorists trying to confuse the two superpowers. Ryan takes great risks to get the information to the president so that he can make accurate decisions.

By the Book

Proverbs 2:12-15; 3:5-6; John 16:33; 2 Timothy 1:8; 4:5

Where to take it

- Has there ever been a time in your life when you felt as if you were the only one with the information necessary to settle a dispute? How did you handle that situation?

- Think about your faith. You have "information" to give to others. Are you someone who takes risks to tell people about your knowledge of God? When have you done this? Has someone taken risks to tell you about the love of God?

- Both the American and Russian leaders based their decisions on fear and lack of information. On what do you base the decisions you make? In your life, what were the results of making decisions without the right information?

- Jack Ryan was able to see the truth when everyone else was in the dark because he had studied the methods of the Russian president. As Christians, why do you think it's important that we understand how our adversary, Satan, works? What kinds of destruction can we avoid by knowing how he operates and how to counter the moves he makes against us?

- Can you see parallels between Jack's role in this movie and your role on earth? What are they?

Sweet Home Alabama

Trailer

What have you left unsaid to the
people you love?

The movie   romantic comedy, PG-13

Melanie Carmichael (Reese Witherspoon) is well on her way to taking the New York fashion industry by storm. She also has a most eligible and kindhearted bachelor, Andrew (Patrick Dempsey), vying for her hand in marriage. When he proposes, Jack doesn't know that Melanie is still married to her high-school sweetheart whom she left in Alabama over seven years ago. Melanie goes back home to try to get her husband, Jake (Josh Lucas), to give her a divorce. Melanie soon discovers that Jake won't cooperate with her plans to erase their past. The longer she stays in her hometown, the more Melanie realizes that no matter how well she may have reinvented herself in New York City, the life that brings her the most happiness is the one she tried to leave in Pigeon Creek.

This clip   (about 4 minutes)

(**Warning:** The words "hell of a" are in this clip.)

▶ **Start** / 1:04:03 / Melanie Carmichael walks down
Main Street toward the dog cemetery.

■ **Stop** / 1:08:23 / "I'm just sorry I never danced with
you at our wedding."

Melanie's trip back to her hometown begins to open old wounds she thought had healed long ago. When she is out one night, she walks by the dog cemetery. Her dog passed away while she was in New York City, and she takes the opportunity to say goodbye. As she is talking to the headstone, it is clear that much of what she is confessing applies to all the people she had left. She realizes that she was so busy trying to escape her past, to find something new and different, that she abandoned many wonderful people and a good life. While she's in the dog cemetery, Jake arrives and opens the vault of their past.

By the Book

Psalm 34:18; Proverbs 29:23; Ecclesiastes 11:10; John 8:36;
2 Corinthians 7:10; Philippians 2:3-4; James 3:16

Where to take it

? Do you always want more?

? In this scene, Melanie confesses that she ran away from her past and her pain. Is there anything in your life that you try to bury or run away from?

? Melanie got pregnant and had a miscarriage. She tells Jake about the shame she carried because of the relief she felt. She left town soon after in an attempt to escape. Can you share with the group a time you got into a predicament and then felt relieved when nothing happened? How did you find escape?

? Describe a time when you took responsibility and/or faced the consequences of your actions.

? If you had the chance to go back to tell someone "goodbye" and explain how you feel about the way you mistreated him or her, what would you say?

? Is there anyone in your life you need to "get right" with? What does the Bible say about making amends?

? Melanie asks Jake why the truth has to be so complicated. Do you think the truth is always more complicated than running away? Why or why not?

157

Trailer

You may be going the "wrong way."

The movie   comedy, R

Two businessmen trying to get home for Thanksgiving are delayed by the effects of a fierce winter storm. Continually thrown together through a series of comic mishaps, Neal (Steve Martin) and Del (John Candy) find themselves struggling to maintain civility as their very different personalities collide. Rigid and uptight, Neal is irritated by Del's endless eccentricities. The tension escalates as their initial politeness wears thin, and their true feelings are revealed by the frustrations of their trip.

This clip (about 2 minutes)

▶ **Start** / 1:00:00 / "Some joker wants to race."

■ **Stop** / 1:02:33 / "We can laugh about it now. We're all right."

Neal and Del are heading down the highway in the middle of the night trying to get home for Thanksgiving. They pass another car, and the occupants try to tell Neal and Del that they are going the wrong way, that they are driving on the wrong side of the road. Del dismisses the warnings as if the other people are the ones who have the problem. When their car passes between two large 18-wheeler trucks and the two men realize they are in big trouble, Del seems to morph into the devil right before Neal's eyes. When they finally make their way to safety, their personalities clash yet again as the two read the situation very differently.

By the Book

2 Samuel 11-12; Psalm 1:1; 27:11; Proverbs 14:12; Ezekiel 3:21; Matthew 7:13; Luke 17:3

Where to take it

❓ Has there been a time in your life when people told you, "You're going the wrong way," but you just wouldn't listen? Describe the outcome.

❓ Read 2 Samuel 11 and 12. Here we find King David not listening to God's warnings. What were the consequences? What do you think are some of the consequences when people disobey God's will today, in the 21st century?

❓ As the traveling duo go between the two large trucks, Del suddenly becomes "the devil," laughing all the way to their doom. Have you ever had a former friend who wasn't good for you morally? Where do you think you'd be if you stayed in that relationship?

❓ In a way, the people who warned Neal and Del were trying to hold them accountable. Read Ezekiel 3:21 and Luke 17:3. Who, in your life, holds you accountable? What are the reasons you need people like this in your life?

❓ When they are safe, Del looks at the wreck, saying that it's not that bad, and they can laugh about it now because they came out of it all right. Have you ever been a situation where you were a "wreck" on the inside, but you rationalized it and laughed it off? How did this help or hurt you?

Tuck Everlasting

Trailer

What does the unlived life look like?

The movie   drama, PG

Winnie Foster (Alexis Bledel), a young girl with an adventurous spirit, is constantly being reigned in by her upper-class, snobbish parents. When Winnie is told that she is being sent away to finishing school, she escapes into the woods where she encounters Jesse Tuck (Jonathon Jackson) and his family. The Tuck family has been around for more than a century because they discovered a spring whose waters give eternal life on earth to anyone who drinks from it. They decide to keep Winnie with them until she can be trusted with their secret. While there, Winnie begins to fall in love with Jesse and soon has her own life or death choice to make.

This clip   (just under 2 minutes)

▶ **Start** / 0:57:00 / Rowboats on the lake.

■ **Stop** / 0:59:25 / "Be afraid of the unlived life."

The patriarch, Angus Tuck (William Hurt), takes Winnie on a boat ride into the middle of the lake to talk about the choice before her: Winnie can either drink from the spring, staying the same age and spending forever on earth with Jesse, or choose not to drink, growing old and leaving her new love behind. Trying to explain to Winnie how he and his family are stuck, remaining the same while the rest of the world changes around them, Mr. Tuck talks to her about death and life. He says the only thing that is unnatural and truly sad is never to ever experience either one.

By the Book

John 3:3-6; Romans 6:9, 23; 8:13; 14:8; 1 Corinthians 15:26;
1 Peter 2:24

Where to take it

? Tuck says that death is just a part of life. Why do you think this is so difficult for us to accept? What do Romans 6:9, 6:23, and 14:8 say about death?

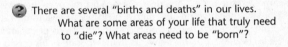

? There are several "births and deaths" in our lives. What are some areas of your life that truly need to "die"? What areas need to be "born"?

? Tuck tells Winnie, "Don't be afraid of death; be afraid of the unlived life." What does this statement mean to you?

? Read John 3:3-6. Explain what it means to be "born again."

? Tuck tells Winnie that the members of his family are like rocks stuck on the side of the stream, forever unchanged and unchanging as the rest of the world moves on by. Is this good? In what ways do you want to stay the same as you are now? Do you know any adults who have been "stuck" in certain areas since they were in high school or college?

? Tuck says that many people try to find ways not to die and many people make excuses not to live their lives. Which description more closely describes you? Why?

Tucker: The Man and His Dream

Trailer

Have you ever had dreams that
other people followed?

The movie — drama, PG

Preston Tucker (Jeff Bridges) is an innovative automobile designer who dreams of making the perfect American car. Against the odds, he moves from his barn to a large factory and sets out to build his new automobile. The big three automakers realize that it would cost them billions of dollars to keep up with the innovations that Tucker wants to incorporate in his cars, and they pull out all the stops to crush him. Forced to dig deep into his spirit, Tucker must decide what he will do to keep his dreams alive.

This clip (just under 3 minutes)

▶ **Start** / 1:12:32 / "What's all this cloak and dagger business?"

■ **Stop** / 1:15:30 / Abe hugs Tucker.

Abe Karatz (Martin Landau) partners with Tucker in the mission to create a better automobile. When the car starts to get noticed, Abe gives Tucker his resignation papers. Taken aback because they have come so far together, Tucker knows there must be more to what Abe is doing. Reluctantly, Abe admits he has never wanted anything more than to be a part of something great, but he doesn't want his prison record to hurt Tucker's reputation. Tucker assures Abe that he can handle his past. Abe is overwhelmed by the grace Tucker gives him and for his faith in their future together.

By the Book

Job 33:14-17; Proverbs 29:18; Luke 9:23; Acts 2:17; 1 Corinthians 13:5; Ephesians 1:7

Where to take it

❓ Have you ever had a dream that was bigger than you, that involved others? Did you pursue it? If so, did people follow?

❓ Abe resigns from being a part of this huge dream because of his past. He doesn't want Tucker to go down because of something he did. Have your past mistakes ever caused you to leave someone so that person wouldn't get hurt by your past actions?

❓ What is the one big dream you have for your life? What kind of obstacles would you be willing to face to achieve this dream? What wouldn't you be willing to face to achieve your dream? How would this change if you knew your dream was a part of God's will?

❓ Ralph Waldo Emerson said, "The mass of men lead lives of quiet desperation." What does this mean to you? Do you think it is a true statement? What do you think will keep you from living a life of "quiet desperation"?

❓ Read Job 33:14-17 and Acts 2:17. How does God give us visions and dreams?

❓ Abe admits he started the venture with Tucker in order to make money. He didn't realize he would be become passionate about something bigger than himself. What can you do with your friends to make a difference that is bigger than all of you?

Unbreakable

The movie   drama, PG-13

David Dunn (Bruce Willis) is a security guard who leads a fairly simple life until the day he emerges from a train wreck as the sole survivor. He begins to question how he managed to come through without a scratch when everyone else around him perished. Instead of feeling grateful for being alive, he is burdened by a responsibility he is unsure he wants. Following the crash, a mysterious man named Elijah Price (Samuel L. Jackson) contacts David and questions him about his medical history. Elijah is a comic book fanatic who suffers from a genetic disorder that makes his bones so brittle that they shatter under the slightest of pressure. Elijah is convinced that he and David share a bizarre connection as men on the opposite ends of the spectrum of strength. He also believes that comic heroes walk the earth and that David, who seems to be unbreakable, could be one of them.

This clip   (about 5 minutes)

▶ **Start** / 0:44:45 / David Dunn is lifting weights.

■ **Stop** / 0:49:50 / "About 350 pounds."

With his son, Joseph (Spencer Treat Clark), David goes down to the bench press in his basement to test his strength. After doing a couple of repetitions with a large amount of weight on the bar, David asks his son how much weight he put on the bar. It is more than David has ever lifted. David allows his son to keep adding on weight to test the limits of his physical stamina. At first, he is hesitant about letting his son see the extent of his power, but soon, they are both amazed by what seems to be his unlimited hidden strength.

By the Book

Psalm 46:1; 71:7; Acts 1:8; 2 Corinthians 12:10; 13:5; 1 Peter 2:2-5

Where to take it

? If your spiritual life were compared to muscle strength, on a scale of 1 to 10 (10 being the strongest), how strong are you?

? Have you ever tested yourself spiritually? How did you measure yourself? Were you encouraged or discouraged by your spiritual strength?

? Read 1 Peter 2:2-5. In what ways do you work to build yourself spiritually? What are some of the benefits of "working out" spiritually?

? Do you think that you can you lose "spiritual muscle"? Explain why or why not.

? David is fascinated that he can lift so much weight. What are some times in your life when you were taken by surprise because God's power helped you to accomplish more than you thought you could?

? What are some areas of your life that you haven't let God's power strengthen you so you can make a difference?

The movie drama, PG

Landon (Shane West) is a popular but unmotivated high school senior who
gets in trouble when a prank injures another classmate. Thinking that it's time
Landon interact with some new people in his life, his principal sentences the
young man to tutoring kids and joining the drama group for the spring
play...neither is exactly cool in Landon's book. In these activities, Landon
meets a new crowd, and his life begins to change, mostly through his
friendship with Jamie Sullivan (Mandy Moore). The daughter of a Baptist
minister, Jamie is not trendy or popular, but there's something real about her
that begins to attract Landon. As he delves deeper into Jamie's world, Landon
discovers that she makes him want to be a better person. As their relationship
develops, both must walk the road of unconditional love.

This clip (about 2 minutes)

▶ **Start** / 0:16:04 / Landon puts a CD into the player.

■ **Stop** / 0:18:15 / Bus driving down road.

Jamie and Landon are riding the bus back into town from tutoring. Jamie likes
to help the younger students, but Landon is just serving his punishment. On
the ride home, Jamie begins to talk with Landon about one of the kids he's
trying to help, but he brushes her off. He tries to let her know what he thinks
about the way she looks, how she acts, and what she believes is important.
However, Jamie is not influenced by his shallow understanding of her or his
attempt to intimidate her.

By the Book

Matthew 5:11; Romans 12:2; 2 Timothy 1:8-9; 2:15; 1 Peter 4:12-16

Where to take it

(?) Jamie Sullivan carries her Bible with her. Do you know anyone like this? Are you like this? Why or why not?

(?) Landon gives Jamie a list of things he's noticed about her over the years. What are some things someone who has known you only from a distance would notice about you? What are your qualities that you would list? Do you think your close friends would agree or disagree with your list?

(?) Landon tells Jamie that she is not a "total reject" but a "self exile." Do you live in a holy huddle, or do you make yourself available to people who need to hear the good news?

(?) Which group do you think is the most judgmental: Christians or non-Christians? Why?

(?) Landon asks if Jamie cares about what people think of her, and she tells him she doesn't. On a scale of 1 to 10 (10 being the greatest), how concerned are you with the opinions of others?

(?) Do you think being a Christian will be easier or more difficult when you are finished with high school?

(?) 2 Timothy 1:8 says, "Do not be ashamed of the gospel of Christ." What do you think this means on a daily basis? How does that play out in your life?

Prepare for your "battlefield."

The movie drama, R

Lieutenant Colonel Harold Moore (Mel Gibson) is assigned to train a division of soldiers to get deep within enemy territory by helicopter. After teaching his troops to be a new kind of cavalry, his unit is sent into the first major battle of the Vietnam War. In the Ia Drang Valley, 395 soldiers from the Air Cavalry are surrounded by more than 4,000 North Vietnamese forces for three days. The American soldiers find themselves drastically outnumbered, but in no way outmaneuvered because of Lt. Col. Moore's leadership and his soldiers' courage. The colonel promises his men that they will either live or die together, and he fights through the agonizing battle, making sure he keeps that promise.

This clip (just under 2 minutes)

▶ **Start** / 0:32:46 / "Look around you...in the seventh cavalry...."

■ **Stop** / 0:35:00 / "So help me God."

Before the troops of the Seventh Air Calvary go to war, Lt. Col. Moore talks to them about fighting for their country, for freedom, and for each other. Moore makes it clear that there will be no racial distinctions among them on the battlefield; they will all walk through the valley of the shadow of death together. Although Lt. Col. Moore clearly states that they are about to fight a ferocious enemy and some may not make it back alive, he promises them that, as their leader, he will be the first one on the battlefield and the last one to leave.

By the Book

Deuteronomy 20:4; Psalm 23; 108:12-13; 139; Isaiah 42:13; 1 Peter 5:8; 2 Peter 2:21

Where to take it

? Lt. Col. Moore talks about going into the valley of shadow of death. Read Psalm 23. What does this Psalm mean to you?

? Lt. Col. Moore tells the men, "We are going into battle against a tough and determined enemy." Read 1 Peter 5:8. How is Satan a tough and determined enemy?

? Do you see dissention in the army of God? Do you think everyone in the army of God is fighting for the same cause?

? Watch this clip through spiritual lenses, thinking of their war as a spiritual battle. How does this change the meaning of the clip for you?

? What does your battlefield look like? How involved are you in the spiritual battle?

? Lt. Col. Moore says that some soldiers won't make it back alive. Do you have friends who began with strong faith but, for some reason, lost interest or stopped caring? What happened?

What Women Want

Trailer

It's time we had..."The Talk."

The movie · romantic comedy, PG-13

Nick Marshall (Mel Gibson) is a guy who appears to have it all—he's charming, successful, and a real man's man. Nick is on his way to the top in his advertising firm...until a woman is hired for the position he thought was his. While trying to figure out how to undermine his new boss, Nick has a freak accident in his bathroom and, the next morning, awakens able to hear what women are thinking. As he seeks to use his new talent to his own advantage, he is surprised at what women really think about life...and about him. Nick begins listening, and what he hears changes how he views and values the opposite sex, which alters his relationships with the women in his life.

This clip (about 2 minutes)

▶ **Start** / 1:17:50 / "I think this is the one."

■ **Stop** / 1:20:24 / "Move on dude, it's over."

While helping his daughter, Alex (Ashley Johnson), shop for a prom dress, Nick discovers that she plans to lose her virginity on prom night. When the two go to lunch afterward, he tries to talk to Alex about sex. The topic itself is challenging enough, but because he has neglected their relationship for years and because she has ideas very different from his, Nick struggles even more than usual through the conversation. He tries to connect with his daughter and give her some guidance.

By the Book

Exodus 20:12; 1 Corinthians 6:18-20; Ephesians 6:1-3; 1 Thessalonians 4:3-4

Where to take it

(?) Describe your relationship with your mom or dad.

(?) Have you ever had "The Talk" with your parents? What was that like?

(?) If you were a parent, what advice would you give to your children about sex?

(?) Nick tells his daughter, "Boys and girls think very differently about sex. My hunch is girls, they just want guys to like them and hang out with them. Whereas guys, and not all guys, but most guys—they pretty much just want to have sex." Do you think this a true statement?

(?) What are some of the reasons you tune out your parents when they try to talk to you about serious matters? Who do you talk to about the more difficult issues and decisions in your life?

(?) Exodus 20:12 mentions "honoring" your mother and father. What does this mean? Do you think Alex honors her father in this clip? Given the kind of parent Nick has been, is she responsible for honoring him?

White Oleander

Trailer
Have you accepted Christ as
your personal savior?

The movie drama, PG-13

Astrid Magnusson (Alison Lohman) is a young girl who is being raised by her self-absorbed, artist mother, Ingrid (Michelle Pfeiffer). Astrid's life is completely ripped apart when her mother is convicted and sentenced to 35 years in prison for the murder of her boyfriend. Now, as a ward of the state, Astrid is bounced from foster home to foster home. Living with different foster mothers, she is changed by each relationship. This is a reality that deeply troubles her mother who, from behind bars, continues to try to mold her daughter to be just like her. As Ingrid works her powerful and poisonous influence over her child, Astrid loses more and more respect for the mother she has always put on a pedestal. In the end, Astrid must learn how to prevent her mother from further tainting her future.

This clip (about 2 minutes)

▶ **Start** / 0:26:02 / "Do they hurt you?"

⏹ **Stop** / 0:28:16 / "But killing people who don't want you is evil."

Astrid goes to visit her mother in jail for the first time since the trial. At first, the conversation is superficial, but it changes when Ingrid notices that Astrid is wearing a cross, given to her by her foster mother, Starr (Robin Wright Penn). Astrid explains to her mom what she has learned about church, accepting Christ, and being baptized. Because she does not like what's happened to her daughter, Ingrid sets out to regain what she has lost since she's been in prison—control of Astrid. However, Astrid defends what she has come to believe, even telling her mother what she thinks about the evil nature of her actions.

By the Book

Proverbs 16:9; 19:21; John 14:6; Romans 10:9; Galatians 2:20;
1 Peter 1:18-21

Where to take it

? When people wear crosses around their necks, what statement do you think they are making?

? Astrid claims she has been saved. What do you think it means to "accept Jesus Christ as your personal Lord and Savior"? Read John 14:6 and Romans 10:9. What do you think it takes to be a true believer of Christ? Do you think there are many ways to accept Jesus?

? In this clip, Astrid and her mother discussed being "washed in the blood of the lamb." Read 1 Peter 1:18-21. After reading this passage, what do you think it means to be "washed in the blood of the lamb"?

? Astrid and her mother argue about being an individual and "thinking for oneself." Astrid claims it is evil to think for oneself, and her mother says it is more of a sin for Astrid not to think for herself. With which character do you find yourself agreeing more? How can a person balance trusting God and working toward an individual goal? Read Proverbs 16:9 and 19:21.

? Have you ever been asked about what you believe? Was it hard for you to give an answer? Why or why not?

? What kind of friction is caused when parents and children believe differently about Jesus? What advice would you give someone in this situation?

With Honors

The movie   comedy/drama, PG-13

Monty Kessler (Brendan Fraser) is a government student at Harvard who is determined to graduate with honors; however, he is struggling with his senior thesis. On his way home one icy evening, Monty trips and drops the only copy of his paper into the basement boiler room of the library, which happens to be the makeshift shelter of a homeless man, Simon Wilder (Joe Pesci). Simon refuses to return the paper without getting some benefits in return (i.e., food and shelter). Unwillingly, the two men develop a relationship that ultimately teaches them both a great deal about life. Monty learns more from Simon than any thesis assignment could ever teach him, and he becomes more concerned about character and compassion than making the Dean's List.

This clip   (about 4 1/2 minutes)

▶ **Start** / 1:00:00 / The words "St. Peter's Church" pan across the screen.

■ **Stop** / 1:04:39 / "There's nothing to do but wait. I'm sorry."

Monty is concerned that Simon has nowhere else to go and sets out to look for him. When he knocks on the big church doors at St. Peter's and inquires about Simon, Monty is assured by the priest that there hasn't been shelter at the church for years, and the priest directs him to the alley behind the church. Monty finds Simon in bad shape and decides to get him help. When he learns that Simon is very ill and doesn't have long to live, Monty wants to make sure Simon's last days are filled with love and shelter.

By the Book

Matthew 25:31-46; Acts 20:35; 1 Thessalonians 5:14; Hebrews 4:16; 13:2; 1 John 3:17

Where to take it

② Have you ever gone out of your way to help someone? Tell the group about a time when you put your faith into action to help someone else.

② Do you find it ironic that Monty went to the church but found no shelter there? In what ways do you—and in what ways does your youth group—fail to provide a safe place for those who need refuge? How can you change that?

② Describe a time when someone helped you in your time of need. How did that make you feel?

② What do you think it means to be "Jesus with skin on"? What are some ways you can be Jesus to someone?

② Monty takes time to listen to Simon's story. When was the last time you stopped to hear about someone else's life? Why is it so important that someone else really knows us?

② In Matthew 25:31-46, what does Jesus say about serving? What does he say about people who call him "Lord" but do nothing in his name?